~ BEFORE THE LAKE ~

BEFORE THE LAKE

MEMORIES OF THE CHEW VALLEY

EDITOR
LESLEY ROSS

CONTRIBUTING AUTHORS
ANDREW SANDON, LESLEY ROSS, DINAH READ,
DEREK FISHER

MAPS
JEAN ELLIOT

ADDITIONAL RESEARCH
ANDREA CALDWELL, JEAN ELLIOT, BRENDA WHITE

THE HARPTREE
HISTORY SOCIETY

2004

First published in Great Britain 2004

PUBLISHED BY:
The Harptree History Society

© The Harptree History Society

Designed & produced in the UK by ASAP 01275 393 919

ISBN 0-9548832-0-9

PRINTED AND BOUND IN UK BY
Antony Rowe Ltd, Chippenham, Wiltshire

Cover map reproduced from the 1904 Ordnance Survey Map.

Contents

Acknowledgements

We wish to recognise the help we have had from a huge number of people.

Many locals past and present, some sadly who have died since this project commenced, gave unfailingly of their time, memories, information and photographs. It would be inappropriate to single out individuals and we apologise for anyone inadvertently left out from the list. To you all, thank you very much, without your assistance this book could not have been written:

Gordon Ashford, June Baker, Wilf Beer, Acker Bilk, Bob Bond, Audrey Braine *nee* Wilson, May Camby *nee* Curry, Dick and Olive Chapman *nee* Tibbs, Grace Chappell, Audrey Chidzey, Gwen Clark *nee* Marshall, Edward Cooke, Frank Cook, Cissie Crocker *nee* Marshall, John and Kath Curry, Valerie Dean, Janet Durbin *nee* Wilson, Heather Dury *nee* Wilson, Audrey Edwards *nee* Watts, Walter Fisher, Alfred Gay, James Gay, Walter Goldstone, Richard Groves, Bill Guard, Maurice and Mary Hasell, Brian Holbrow, Ruth Holder *nee* Curry, Margaret Holmes *nee* Sparkes, Pat Huggins *nee* Cox, James King, F John and Bertha King, Ted King, Mrs Lees, Fred Lyons, Roger Lyons, Mrs D Maggs, Vera Joan Maggs, Frank Marshall, Maud Mellish *nee* Mapstone, Joyce Millard, Tom and Kathleen Pow, Prof. Philip Rahtz, Dr John Rawlins, Pete Saunders, Irene Slack *nee* Lawrence, Kelston Sparkes, Derek and Roger Stenner, Ann Summers *nee* Williams, Harold Taviner, Ivy Thorn *nee* Baker, Mary Tout *nee* Whitfield, Violet Tovey, William Tovey, Joyce Trendall, Rosemary Walker, Sheila Weatherall, Joe and Pam Weaver *nee* Tucker, Tom Whish, Emma Whitcombe *nee* Sparkes, Bett Williams *nee* Dury, Mary Woodward, Tom Wyatt, Arthur Young.

We are most grateful to the following museums, libraries, groups and individuals who assisted us in our research:

English Heritage for permission to quote extracts from '*Excavations at Chew Valley Lake, Somerset*', by P A Rahtz and E Greenfield [1977]

Map on cover reproduced by kind permission, from the 1904 second edition 6 inch Ordnance Survey Map, Somerset Sheet 19NW.

Photograph of the Inauguration of the Lake reproduced by kind permission of *Bristol United Press*.

Alison Farrar – Blaise Castle Museum, Gail Boyle – Bristol City Museum, Bristol University Library, Mavis Eddy – Malago Society, David Bromwich – Taunton Local Studies Library.

Jackie Salter and David Hart – Compton Martin History Society, especially for the loan of the C S Fox drawings of Moreton houses.

Jim Ross for the photograph on the back cover.

Martin Bodman, Roly Currell, Ian Durham, David Hoddinott, Margaret Hucker, Barry Huggins, Graham Sage, Trevor Turpin, Sheila Walker.

Chew Magna Monday Club, Compton Martin Lunch Club, Harptree Lunch Club.

We are particularly grateful to Jeremy Williams and Paul Kelson, Corporate Affairs Dept, Bristol Water for their assistance throughout this project and for permission to use Bristol Water publications and photographs.

Many thanks to Dinah Read for the line drawings and to Jeanette Clark for all her support and for doing the difficult but vital task of proof reading.

This publication has been made possible due to a grant from the National Lottery's Awards for All programme.

Introduction

When one looks at the Chew Valley Lake today, surrounded as it is by mature trees, with its fishing, sailing, birds, picnic area and buildings, it is easy to imagine that it has been in existence for much longer than the 50 or so years since the reservoir was constructed. It is also hard to visualise what lay under the flat sheet of water that you see now, to picture the contours of the land, how the land was used, the buildings and lanes, the river and its bridges and tributary streams. More importantly, what was life like for the people who lived there?

It is the purpose of this book to tell the story of this part of what is now known as the Chew Valley and how it interacted with the villages round about. (The 'Chew Valley' as an identifiable community only developed with the arrival of the lake.)

The archaeological excavations at the time of the construction of the reservoir in the 1950s showed that this story started about 12,000 years ago and that Romans also settled here. Anglo-Saxons were followed by Normans, and they and their followers were here in medieval times. From records it is possible to learn something about the area and its people up to the time when living memory takes over. The main part of the story, however, is based on the oral memories of people who lived in and around the valley – many still do. These memories broadly cover the period from the 1930s through to the 1950s and speak of a way of life that is very different from today.

We recorded many interesting memories of the various topics into which the latter part of the book is divided and we have used the voices directly as far as possible. No names are attributed to the individual quotations as the interviews were conducted on the basis of anonymity. Where names are given they are used to enhance or define a place or event or where the knowledge of the originator adds interest to the memory. However, it is only human nature that people may remember the same incident in different ways. With the passage of years not all memories are accurate, they are interpretations, therefore, some readers may well have different recollections.

The earlier historical sections are, of necessity, largely based on documentary evidence or on information from books and other written material, including those by other local historians. Even for the earliest times, however, we were fortunate in being able to speak to the archaeologist who carried out the investigations at the reservoir site.

We have tried to be consistent with the spellings of family and place names, but these varied over the generations. Similarly, agricultural equipment and produce often had more than one spelling – for example, mangold and mangel-wurzel are both correct.

Some more detailed information has been included as appendices – for example, the occupiers of the dwellings that were demolished for the lake at various significant dates. Also found there are the full names for the small number of abbreviations that are used, and the documentary sources for information.

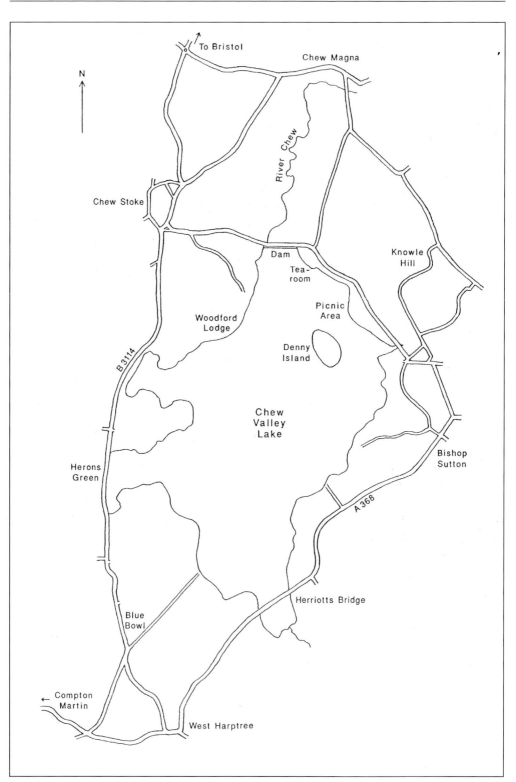

MAP A   THE CHEW VALLEY TODAY

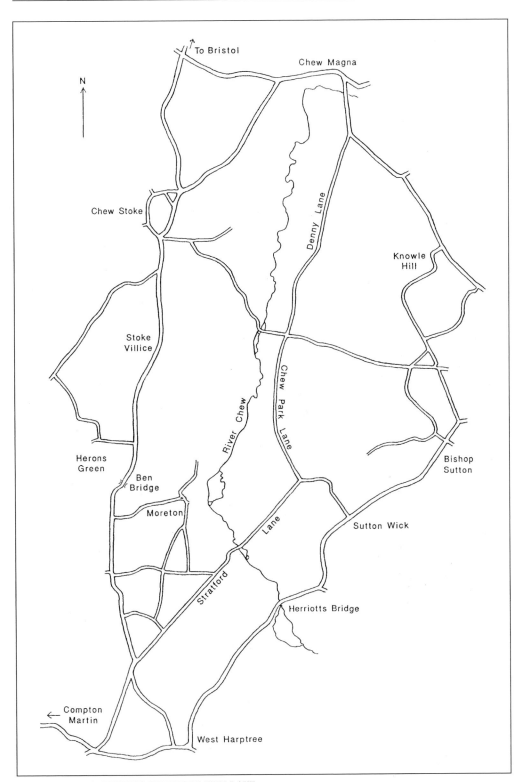

To Bristol

Chew Magna

N

Chew Stoke

Denny Lane

Knowle Hill

Stoke Villice

River Chew

Chew Park Lane

Herons Green

Ben Bridge

Bishop Sutton

Moreton

Sutton Wick

Stratford Lane

Herriotts Bridge

Compton Martin

West Harptree

MAP B   THE CHEW VALLEY BEFORE THE LAKE

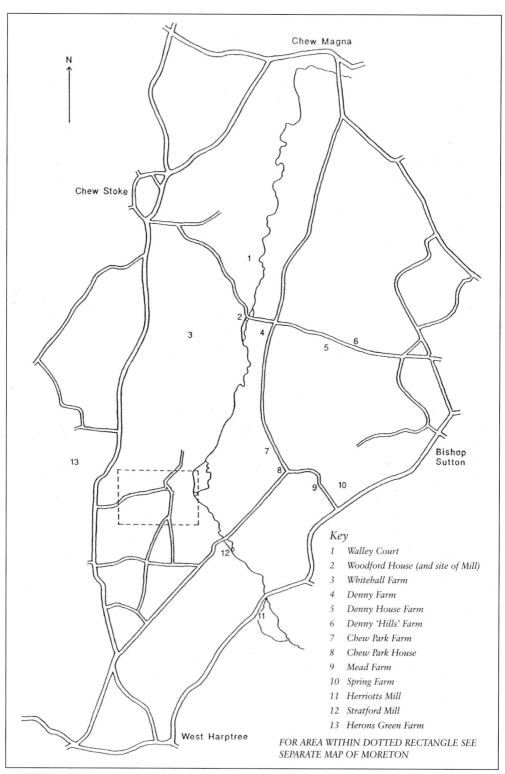

Chew Magna

N

Chew Stoke

1

2

3

4

6

5

Bishop
Sutton

7

13

8

9

10

Key

1	Walley Court
2	Woodford House (and site of Mill)
3	Whitehall Farm
4	Denny Farm
5	Denny House Farm
6	Denny 'Hills' Farm
7	Chew Park Farm
8	Chew Park House
9	Mead Farm
10	Spring Farm
11	Herriotts Mill
12	Stratford Mill
13	Herons Green Farm

12

11

West Harptree

*FOR AREA WITHIN DOTTED RECTANGLE SEE
SEPARATE MAP OF MORETON*

MAP C   LOCATION PLAN OF PROPERTIES

CHAPTER ONE

The Valley as it Was

The landscape of the valley

This part of the valley of the River Chew was not, of course, chosen for the site of the reservoir by accident. Apart from the requirement to deliver sufficient water of drinkable quality, one of its advantages was the narrow gap at the north end where the sides of the valley came together to constrain the Chew to flow between steep banks. This is where the dam is now.

The Chew fell about 35 ft (from 185 ft to 150 ft above sea level) from Herriotts Bridge to the dam site. It flowed generally northwards but with many twists and turns, and was joined by tributary streams, including one flowing from the hills behind what is now Herons Bay, and Hollow Brook joining from the east near the dam. There were four mill leats along the way indicating the sites of mills at Herriotts Bridge, Stratford Lane, Moreton and Woodford. The river kept nearer to the western side of the valley where the valley sides were steeper (particularly as it neared the dam). The river could be a quiet babbling brook in summer, in full flow in spring, and often flooding the low-lying fields and surrounding the buildings close by after heavy rain. Downstream from Moreton the bank was generally lined with undergrowth, while upstream towards Stratford Mill the banks were more open – an important feature for a fly-fisherman. People remember a large variety of wildlife – otters, water voles, kingfishers, moorhens and other birds, dragon flies – and flowers, including kingcups and meadows filled with buttercups and daisies.

To the eastern side of the valley the slope was far more gradual. A schoolgirl of the time, who lived nearer the Chew Stoke end, remembers the advantage of the easy walking to school at Bishop Sutton, rather than having to climb the steep hill to Chew Stoke school. On this side, within the valley, were two small hills. The taller of the two stands above the level of the lake and is now known as Denny Island. The other, further south, was one of the last parts to be flooded and was where the Roman villa was discovered – known to fishermen as Roman Shallows. On the western side, the two places where the water comes up to the present road show where there was a promontory between two small valleys. One extended back into Herons Green and contained the stream that passed under Ben Bridge (still visible at times of drought).

The valley was divided into small to medium sized fields, some still showing the layout of medieval field systems. Almost all the fields were used for meadow or pasture, although there was some arable on the higher, drier ground. The acreage of arable was increased of necessity during World War 2 (WW2). The fields were hedged rather than fenced – elms being the predominant trees. Every farmhouse had its orchard close by. Grass verges full of wild flowers bordered the lanes, with high hedges that sometimes met overhead.

The lanes and the dwellings

The people in the valley either lived in the small community of the hamlet of Moreton – to the south east close to the parking area at Herons Green – or in the farms and cottages scattered about along the narrow lanes. As well as providing access to these dwellings, the lanes were also used as through routes by people mainly on foot, bicycle or all forms of horse transport. The main routes were between Bishop Sutton in the south, and Chew Stoke and Chew Magna in the north, and between Bishop Sutton and Moreton. Other dwellings that were demolished for the reservoir were in Stoke Villice and further to the south along the old road between West Harptree and Chew Stoke.

The lanes and the locations of the dwellings that no longer exist are described in the following paragraphs, with the exception of Moreton, which deserves a separate chapter. The names of the people who lived at various dates in the dwellings that no longer exist can be found in Appendix B.

The lane from Chew Stoke to Bishop Sutton went past the Methodist chapel (which is still there). After about a quarter of a mile it reached a fork.

The left-hand fork, Walley Lane, led eventually into fields and to the drive on the right leading to Walley Court, at the top of the steep slope down to the river. Its site is quite close to where the dam is now and practically at the water's edge. By 1938 it was a farmhouse, although it had been more important in the past.

The right hand fork was the lane to Bishop Sutton and is still identifiable for a short distance. It skirted around Woodford Hill and down the slope to the river where Woodford House, with its cottage, stood on the right. In earlier times Woodford Mill also stood there. On the high ground to the right of the lane, less than half a mile away, was Whitehall Farm which originally had a right of way to this lane. During the 19th century the approach was changed to be via the Chew Stoke to West Harptree road. This now provides the entrance drive to Woodford Lodge. The site of the farm lies to the left as you come into the open space near the lodge. The farm pond is still visible but very overgrown.

At Woodford House, the lane turned eastwards, crossed the Chew by a bridge having a single semi-circular arch, and started the climb towards a small hill (now Denny Island). Shortly afterwards it met and crossed the lane between Chew Magna and Sutton Wick – called Denny Lane here but Chew Park Lane further on towards Sutton Wick. Denny Farm, partly moated, was on the right hand side behind an orchard just before this crossroads, although its entrance was in Denny Lane. In about a quarter of a mile, there was a cottage on the left, inhabited in 1901 but in ruins by 1938. Shortly afterwards, on the hill set back on the right was Denny House Farm, with its cottage in front on the lane. Further along on the left came a third farm also called Denny, known latterly as Denny 'Hills' Farm after the family that lived there. The Hollow Brook ran along the back of the garden. The lane continued to the junction with the lanes leading to Stowey Bottom and Bishop Sutton by the house called Twycross, originally a small farm but with most of its fields taken for the reservoir. One end of the new road round the lake, and across the dam to Chew Stoke is also at this junction.

From Chew Magna to Sutton Wick, at the western end of Bishop Sutton, the route crossed the Tun Bridge over the Chew at Chew Magna and turned right along Denny Lane, as now. At what is now the junction with the new road opposite the tearoom area, Denny Lane carried straight on down the steep slope to the Hollow Brook, which it crossed by the 'White Bridge' – known as such because of its white painted posts. Having passed the crossroads with the Chew Stoke to Bishop Sutton lane and then Denny Farm on the right, the lane continued as Chew Park Lane, as mentioned before. About three-quarters of a mile from the crossroads, on the right, stood Chew

Park Farm and, a short distance further on, Chew Park House.

Chew Park House was at a fork in the road. Directly in front, in the wide 'V' formed by the forks were some long narrow fields set out in a curious fan shape. These probably represented a 'gore' – part of a medieval field system – that still survived. The fork to the right was the Stratford Lane Roman road which crossed the Chew at Stratford Bridge near to Stratford Mill. It passed the lane to Moreton on the right, and a cottage on the left (described in the chapter on Moreton), and then continued up to the Blue Bowl Inn on the main road.

The fork to the left made a couple of bends and in about a quarter of a mile it arrived at three cottages raised up on the right hand side. The first of these was known as Mead Farm. In a short distance, up the track on the left, was Spring Farm, a building with medieval origins. The lane widened to a triangular green (now obscured by trees) as it joined the main Bishop Sutton to West Harptree road at Sutton Wick.

The line of the stretch of the old Chew Stoke to West Harptree road, from Stoke Villice to just beyond Herons Green Bay, ran to the east of the present one over Ben Bridge. One farm was demolished here – Herons Green Farm (not the present farm with the same name), which lay to the west of the present road behind the parking area. The other dwellings demolished were: two houses and two bungalows – all built in the 20th century – to the left of the old road above the junction with Kingshill Lane; and three older cottages on the right of the old road in Stoke Villice itself. Another building worthy of mention was that described, on the Bristol Waterworks (BWW) 1938 map, as a disused artificial manure factory – known locally as 'the stink factory' – which had started life as a milk depot.

The official view and plans for the valley

An official assessment of the Chew Valley area in the 1920s can be found in the 'Bristol and Bath Regional Planning Scheme' which was published in 1930. This document was a response to the Town Planning Act of the time that required all urban authorities with populations of more than 20,000 to prepare plans. After consultation between Bristol and the relevant local authorities, it was agreed that the plan should cover the whole area lying north of the Mendips and west of the Cotswolds, including the Chew Valley.

The report sets out what the situation was at the time and makes proposals on the landscape, economic activities (identified as agriculture and mining), the roads, and on water, sewerage and electricity services.

For the purposes of planning, the landscape was divided into five categories, and the Chew Valley in the surroundings of the future lake site was included in a wider area classified as 'remarkable country'. This was defined as 'land, largely agricultural, which owing to contour, vegetation, water or other causes is of remarkable landscape value'. Mendip itself was classified as 'wild country'. The report commented that:

> *Unfortunately for the continued repose of this area there is coal under the eastern part of it – the first indication of possible change can be seen in a village colliery near Bishop Sutton. One hopes that even coal mining may not destroy this rural beauty.*

The reason for this concern is clear in a map that shows that the lower coal measures extend across the whole of the valley in a band lying north-north-west and in width from Chew Stoke to Chew Magna. The proposals for land use were that the area should be one of 'special landscape reservations' for its landscape amenity value and should be retained in its present form with as little change as is practicable. 'It is not thought possible to limit or prohibit coal mining altogether but it is to be carried out in a more isolated manner (without subsidiary industries) than in the normal agricultural zone.' As it happened, of course, further coal mining was not a profitable commercial undertaking and this concern was misplaced.

It was proposed that a road should be built to by-pass West Harptree on the north side, based on the rising traffic volumes recorded in the 1920s at the census point on the A368 at Sutton Court. These were, in 1922 (167 movements per day), 1925 (401) and 1928 (524). A more ambitious proposal was to provide better access to the coal fields at Midsomer Norton and Radstock. This would have involved a second by-pass to the south side of West Harptree as well as a road upstream of the Litton reservoirs and along Hollowmarsh Lane to Farrington Gurney. Neither scheme materialised. Otherwise it was recommended that, 'The roads should be kept for local use but do nothing to encourage traffic into the area'.

West Harptree and North Widcombe were said to be adequately supplied with water from wells or springs, while Chew Magna, Chew Stoke and East Harptree had inadequate water supplies. West Harptree, Chew Stoke, Chew Magna, Stanton Drew, Pensford and Publow all discharged their sewage directly into the River Chew. It was therefore proposed that 'the Chew Valley villages will find it an economy to provide a combined plant and outfall east of Publow'. Interestingly, no proposals were made about drinking water supplies.

The report also noted that none of the villages surrounding the (present) lake area were either currently served, or capable of being served, by the existing electricity sub-stations. (The engineer living at Woodford House had, however, rigged up a dynamo to generate his own electricity using the river.) It was not proposed that anything should be done about this. The implication was that electric power would open up the area to development, as would any extension of the railway branch line from Blagdon.

CHAPTER TWO

Prehistory and Romans

The project to build the reservoir was the trigger for the archaeological excavations that started during the construction in 1953 and ended two years later when the water rose to cover all the sites. The archaeologists (employed by the Ministry of Works) who carried out most of the excavations were Philip Rahtz and his colleague Ernest Greenfield. They were helped with the digging by four paid labourers (including one local farmer) and, at Chew Park, by 30-40 volunteers. We were fortunate to have the opportunity of speaking to Philip Rahtz himself in preparing this book and he was able to give us some personal memories to enliven the official record of the work. The voice you hear in this chapter is his.

The Stratford Lane Roman road was the only significant site known in the early 1950s – although a trial dig had been carried out by Mr F C Jones of BWW in 1949, at a site near Whitehall Farm known locally as Nunnery Fields. Some medieval remains, believed then to be of a small nunnery, had been discovered there.

Originally I was only engaged for a week or two to dig this Roman road and then of course we went on continuously for two years.

The history of the valley was virtually a blank before that and written off as archaeologically barren. It was in fact a wonderful sample of everything from about 10,000 BC onwards. And so the most interesting thing was to have a piece of landscape of 1200 acres whose history could be taken from the earliest prehistory right the way through to the flooding. It was the first time that anybody in England had actually done a whole landscape. The two years in the Chew Valley was the equivalent of a lifetime of experience because every period was represented and different kinds of sites. You wouldn't get such an opportunity now, over two years, to find out about archaeology.

The plant and machinery used by BWW to clear the vegetation and to scrape the top layer of soil exposed the initial evidence of possible early occupation – over a far larger area and far more quickly than traditional methods would have done – although laborious hand digging was still needed afterwards.

When we were digging the Roman road with a trench across it, workmen came over from Herriotts Bridge and said, 'Oh you chaps should be over there'. Other things were turning up there, skeletons and pottery. So we straight away dropped what we were doing and went over, and there was the site of Herriotts Bridge all stripped by the Water Works – a lovely dry pond. And of course all the red clay had been exposed over fifteen acres and there was a huge Roman site, so the whole thing took on a very different complexion then.

Eight separate sites were excavated within the lake area: at Chew Park (near Chew Park Farm); Herriotts Bridge; Ben Bridge; Moreton; St Cross Nunnery (near Whitehall Farm); Stratford Mill; Stratford Lane; and Denny Moat (near Denny House Farm). Other sites excavated as part of the overall reservoir scheme – but outside the scope of this book – were the Roman villa at Golds Cross and other sites along the routes of various pipelines. Some excavation work was also carried out at Burledge Camp above North Widcombe.

The results of the work, and that of the many experts that examined, identified and interpreted the features, objects, soil and pollen samples etc., are set out by Philip Rahtz and Ernest Greenfield in their book 'Excavations at Chew Valley Lake, Somerset'. Due to the vast scale of the excavations, a large number of experts were needed to record and identify the various finds and it was twenty years before the book was published by the Department of the Environment (the successor to the Ministry of Works) in 1977.

For the general reader, probably the most interesting aspects of the book are the conclusions reached from interpreting the findings, about the people of those early times.

It was quite exciting because, when you get into archaeology, you realise that all the finds like the copper jug and the pewter jug are very nice, but what you are really interested in are what they tell you about the people that lived there.

This chapter draws its information almost entirely from the book, concentrating on the period from about 10,000 BC to the end of the Roman settlement around the middle of the 4th century AD. For this period, the most important sites were at Chew Park, Herriotts Bridge and, to a lesser extent, Ben Bridge.

Those who wish to know more should read the book itself, which is the comprehensive and definitive work on the subject, bearing in mind that further analysis, which could update the findings of the book, may well have been published since. The prehistoric and Roman remains discovered are all held by the Bristol City Museum.

The prehistoric period

The prehistoric period was from about 10,000 BC until 'romanisation' around the middle of the 1st century AD. The excavations found evidence of people belonging to the consecutive periods known as Upper Palaeolithic, Mesolithic and Neolithic (Old, Middle and New Stone Ages), Bronze Age and Iron Age. For comparison, the stone circles of Stanton Drew are dated broadly to the late Neolithic and early Bronze Ages at about 3000 to 2000 BC. The wood circles or henges discovered there would be even earlier. In England, the Iron Age is dated from perhaps about 500 BC.

For the Upper Palaeolithic and Mesolithic periods, various stone implements were found. These included a knife at Herriotts Bridge; a number of flint blades at Chew Park, similar to those found in the Mendip caves; and the head of a mace at Moreton. No evidence was found, however, that the people actually settled in the valley.

Firm evidence of occupation in the Neolithic period was only found at Chew Park: a ring of post holes for a small circular hut or house about ten feet in diameter, and a small pit containing fragments of pottery and flint and other domestic refuse (perhaps used originally for storage). The hut was likely to have been a temporary shelter – perhaps for a herdsman – rather than a more permanent dwelling. Another possible storage pit, also containing pottery sherds and other rubbish, was found at Ben Bridge but no evidence of a hut. Other tools, including fragments of polished flint axes (but unfortunately no complete ones) were found at other sites.

Chew Park and Ben Bridge are also the main sites where Bronze Age features were found. At Chew Park a circular grave dated of around 1800 BC was discovered. This contained the burnt bones of a man aged perhaps 30 years old when he died. From the various tools, pottery sherds and other items – including a flat stone quern for grinding corn – in the grave, it was concluded that these had come from a site where people lived rather than being specially made grave goods. The quern was of special interest, as it was the earliest evidence of cereal cultivation in the valley. A similar pit was found at Ben Bridge, although this one contained no bones. As the contents included a small wrist guard, probably made of slate, it was considered that, on balance, this was also probably a grave rather than a rubbish pit. A scatter of flints was also found at most of the sites that were examined.

With the Iron Age, it was possible to identify three separate phases of settlement in the area. At Chew Park the first phase was represented by a long straight ditch and several pits, which were thought to represent either the fringe of a farmstead or an outlying granary or barn connected with a farm. For the second phase, features of a pair of circular timber houses with internal posts supporting the roof were discovered, together with a dump of broken cooking pots. One of the two houses had been built partially on the site of the other one and therefore could either have been built as a direct replacement of the first or some time later. In the third phase, a rectangular pattern of small post holes were interpreted as granaries raised on stilts above the ground. There was also 'a rather haphazard ditch system' cutting across the sites of the earlier houses, which indicated an attempt at drainage for crop growing.

Similar drainage ditches to those at Chew Park were also found at Herriotts Bridge and Moreton, which, together with pottery found in all three sites, enabled these to be dated to the third Iron Age phase. The pottery from Herriotts Bridge was more obviously made by throwing on a wheel than that from Chew Park – possibly because the people at Herriotts Bridge had mastered this technique better. Similar pottery found at Burledge Camp suggested that the hill fort might have been the focal point for the community to which the open settlements in the valley also belonged.

The Roman period

The transition of the settlements in the valley from the Iron Age to the Roman period was gradual. The transition started in about the second half of the 1st century AD and was complete by the end of that century. The Roman period lasted until about the middle of the 4th century, when the barbarian invasions occurred. The excavations concentrated on the two main sites of Chew Park and Herriotts Bridge. From these, an excellent picture of life at this period was derived and summarised in the record.

The environment was said to be similar to that of the 1950s although more marshy, with periodic flooding of the river and slight changes in its course. The Roman villa that was discovered at Chew Park was sited on a sandy promontory as close to the river as possible without being too wet. The woodland near the villa was predominantly oak and ash, with hazel scrub, hawthorn and fruit trees. Close by, varieties of wheat and barley (including the naked form) were grown.

Fallow deer (larger than the modern breed) lived nearby and the inhabitants kept domestic fowl, dogs and horses. Their diet was vegetable, supplemented by beef and some pork and mutton (also farmed) and by shellfish and snails.

The inhabitants of Herriotts Bridge, both male and female, were big-boned and muscular, especially in the forearms. Their thigh bones were developed through constant climbing up the hills. The people who lived at Chew Park cared for their teeth by picking and polishing with a cleaning agent, and they used a bronze implement to extract them when they became diseased. People imported objects from the north of England and from the continent.

Local materials were used: stone in buildings (from the quarry at Denny Moat), and for tools and grinding equipment – old red sandstone was used for whetstones; coal was used domestically and for industry; limestone was burnt; galena was mined nearby. Basic industries included: glass making; iron smelting; casting an alloy of copper and lead at Chew Park; working galena at Chew Park and Herriotts Bridge, primarily for its silver content but also for lead; and making other metal alloys. Craftsmanship was high, as evidenced by the metal vessels found, the use of axes, adzes and saws for structural, domestic and decorative woodworking, rope made from twisted flax to draw water from the well, and leatherwork – mainly for shoes.

Evidence of ditch digging at Chew Park and Herriotts Bridge during the early Roman period, to drain the valley and bring more land into cultivation, indicated an increase of economic activity. As the valley was the nearest fertile land, this activity was possibly associated with the need to supply food for the people at the Mendip lead mines, via the Stratford Lane Roman road. A large rectangular timber house (or possibly a barn) of around the early Roman period was discovered at Chew Park. The fact that the support posts had been renewed at least once indicated that the building must have been in use for a considerable time, well into the 2nd century. It appears to have been the nucleus of the early romanised occupation of Chew Park. At Herriotts Bridge there was also evidence of settled occupation then (post holes for small huts and other structures, pottery and querns for grinding corn) but no large building.

By the 2nd century full romanisation of the valley had taken place. The drainage ditch systems at Chew Park and Herriotts Bridge were fully developed bringing 30 acres directly into cultivation. Indications of Roman occupation were also found at Moreton, Ben Bridge, St Cross Nunnery and Denny Moat. It was thought probable that most of the valley could have been brought into use at this period.

From the late 2nd century onwards, the fortunes of the Herriotts Bridge people down by the river and the Chew Park people on the higher promontory seem to have diverged. At Herriotts Bridge there were small tent sites (one or two post holes) and hearths. This indicated a subsistence level of occupation and that the site was possibly only used for short periods. Four graves were found: two males of well over 21, a female in late adolescence and a child.

By contrast, at Chew Park in the 3rd century there were signs of small scale industrial activity – iron smelting, a lime kiln and the quarry at Denny Moat. A villa was built solidly of stone on good foundations by early in the 4th century and probably used as a farmhouse. Although the villa was not luxurious, from the evidence of coins and other finds, its owner would have been reasonably wealthy. There were no signs (such as extensions or modifications) that the villa was used for more than one generation of the original family. There were, however signs of 'secondary squalid occupation' for a short time afterwards before abandonment not much later than 350AD. The remaining obvious evidence of the villa's existence would have been removed when the stones from the ruins disappeared into the kilns of the medieval lime burners.

The villa had a good water supply provided by a well, and it was here that one of the most important finds was made, being the first discovered in this country.

The most exciting thing was the discovery of the writing tablets. They have rather been overtaken, because quite a lot of other writing tablets have been found since, especially at Vindolanda. When Ernest was down the well, he sent up a bucket and he said, 'I think this is a writing tablet'. When it came up on the bucket in bright sunshine I could see there was writing on it. We realised that it all might have faded away in the sunshine and so it was hastily put back in the wet mud and sent straight away to London.

After being deciphered some time later, the writing proved to be part of a legal document about the transfer of land – perhaps for the villa itself, though this could not be proved.

After the Romans left

Following the Roman withdrawal in the 4th century, no evidence was found of the use of the valley during the next seven centuries – the 'Dark Ages' and the Anglo-Saxon period. This is not to say that there was not evidence to be found at other unexplored sites.

There are probably a great many more sites under the water. And of course those are fairly safe now.

However, many interesting medieval sites were excavated, particularly at Moreton. These discoveries form part of the continuing history in the next chapter.

CHAPTER THREE

Anglo-Saxons and Middle Ages to 19th Century

We know that the Anglo-Saxons were at Moreton before the arrival of the Normans because we are told this in the Domesday Book that they compiled. In order to bridge the large gap from the Normans to the 20th century and personal memories, we must rely on written records of various sorts, including maps. Once again, however, we have the work of Philip Rahtz and his colleagues, covering the excavations of medieval Moreton and the other medieval sites, to help us.

It is not the intention of this chapter to attempt an exhaustive history of this long period, but rather to mention some of the people, the buildings they lived in and the events (some authoritative, some local folklore) to give a flavour of what life might have been like. The industries of the four mills that this stretch of the River Chew supported were important activities and these are discussed in a separate chapter. Farming remained the most important activity, sometimes prosperous and sometimes less so, responding to climate change and the development of improved techniques. The landscape of the 1930s still bore traces of medieval field systems. Teasels for the cloth trade were grown in the 18th and 19th centuries and by one person at least in the early 20th century.

From the Domesday Book which was completed in 1086, we know who were the chief lords that held the estates that were to be affected by the construction of the reservoir over 850 years later. We use the names of the parishes as they are known today. Compton Martin, which included the manor of Moreton, and Chew Stoke (together comprising the western side) were both held by Serlo de Burci. He was from Calvados in Normandy and held several estates in Somerset – some directly from the King (including Blagdon and Ubley) and some as a tenant of the Bishop of Wells. On the eastern side, Chew Magna (including Bishop Sutton, which was split off in the middle of the 20th century and combined with Stowey to form a separate parish) was held directly by the Bishop of Wells. To the south, West Harptree later incorporated the tithing of North Widcombe, which at Domesday was part of Chewton Mendip and was held by the King. West Harptree itself was split into two manors, one held by Walter de Douai (a Fleming who had been given many estates in Somerset, particularly along the River Parret), and the other by the Bishop of Coutances, also a major land holder in Somerset. These manors were later identified as West Harptree Gournay and West Harptree Tilly respectively.

Moreton

The manor of Moreton was the only significant centre of population at that time within the area of the lake. The Normans, of course, took over a Saxon settlement, although we do not know when it first came into existence. Domesday Book tells us that, in the time of Edward the Confessor, Moreton was split into three manors held equally by three Saxon thanes called Alvric, Aelric and Alwic. Moreton was taxed for five hides – a hide being a flexible measurement, depending on its quality, of the area of land needed to support one free family. Under Serlo de Burci, the people directly holding the land were Godric and Elric, with two hides each. The fifth hide was split between Richard (three quarters) and Humphrey (one quarter), and a total of 27 other people worked on the manor. There were 58 acres of meadow, nineteen acres of woodland and two acres of pasture. There was also a mill paying five shillings. The total value of the manor was said to be £3 15s, both formerly and at the Domesday survey.

Although he was recorded as the holder of Compton Martin (including Moreton) and Chew Stoke, Serlo de Burci apparently died around 1086 during the Domesday Survey. His estates therefore passed to his daughter Geva (his sole heiress as her sister had previously entered the nunnery at Shaftesbury) and, through her, eventually to her son, Robert FitzMartin, by her first husband Martin. As Martin had died before Serlo, and Robert was still under age, the temporary owner for a few years, in right of his wife, was Geva's second husband William de Falaise.

Robert FitzMartin was an important person of the time and made gifts to religious houses and is mentioned in many documents. He supported the Empress Maud against King Stephen as did many of the barons in this part of the country.

The head of his 'barony' of several manors was the manor of Blagdon – presumably the most important of his in the area. He lived until the 1150s and his direct heirs continued for almost another 200 years. They simplified their family surname to Martin along the way and it is preserved in Compton Martin, and also in Combe Martin in Devonshire where the Martins had estates.

The manor of Moreton was held under the feudal system by the 'de Moreton' family (one of the many variations in spelling their name) from the FitzMartins/Martins. As the principal landowners there, they followed a fairly common practice of the time by taking their name from the manor – another local example being the 'de Harptrees'. The de Moretons flourished and they are regularly mentioned in documents up until the middle of the 14th century. There is then a gap of some years after which the manor passes through various hands. The reason for this is uncertain. Possible reasons that have been suggested are that: the Black Death that occurred at that time may have wiped out the inhabitants; local climate change may have made the low-lying Moreton too wet for agriculture; or the lords of the manor may no longer have lived there.

One of the de Moreton family, Thomas de Moreton, was holding the manor of Moreton from William Martin in 1284-85. His effigy – a horizontal full-length figure carved from stone in bas-relief – can be seen in St Michael's Church at Compton Martin. This dates from the late 13th century. The effigy was originally discovered during restoration of the church in 1858 and was poorly restored at that time. However, the Wells Conservation Centre carried out professional conservation work in the late 1980s, after which the effigy was returned to its original location in the church.

An idea of the financial standing of the de Moretons in 1327 can be seen from the records of the 'Lay Subsidy' of that date to raise tax for Edward III. This tax was levied on each person whose goods were of the value of 10s or more, at one-twentieth of the moveable goods (with certain exceptions) in their possession on Michaelmas day of that year. In the record for Compton Martin and Moreton, John de Moreton was assessed at 2s 6d, the next highest amount after John Wake, lord of Compton Martin, who was assessed at 4s. It is interesting to note that the record for West Harptree, whose total tax assessment was double that of Compton and Moreton, includes 'Walterus de Stratforde 2s' (of Stratford Mill). The de Moretons seem to have been on friendly terms with their neighbours at the Harptrees, being witnesses over the years to documents of Robert de Gournay, Anselm de Gournay and Thomas Ap Adam, for example.

The excavations at Moreton revealed the sites of a number of medieval buildings. The chapel was the most important of these and was near Cross (or Laurel) Farm by the crossroads in the centre of Moreton and near the site of the cross referred to below. This was identified as the chapel of St James, which is referred to in a contemporary document. Ralph de Salopia, Bishop of Bath and Wells gave licence in 1332 for 'John de Morton and Alice de Morton his wife' to have divine services celebrated for five years. As no graveyard was discovered there it appears that Compton Martin church still retained this function. During the demolition of Grove Farm in Moreton a carved stone was recovered from the wall of the cow house, which was thought to have been the head of a window from an ecclesiastical building and so might have come from this chapel.

Men working on the archaeological dig near Moreton House (Tibbs Cottage)

The site of a substantial house, suggested to be possibly a manor house of the 12th/13th centuries, was found to the west of the village towards the main road, which would suggest that the de Moretons did live in Moreton at that time. Other sites of medieval buildings found were that of the mill, considered to be the successor to the one mentioned in Domesday, and a number of houses said to be peasants' cottages. It is of interest that Philip Rahtz noted that the sites of the manor house and of one of the other houses were outside the area to be flooded and that BWW had agreed to preserve these sites as pasture or for other normal agricultural use.

A significant landmark in medieval Moreton would have been the cross that stood at the crossroads in the centre of the hamlet. By the middle of the 20th century all that remained in place was the large square stone that would have formed the lowest level of the base. A chance sighting of what seemed to be an unusual coping stone used for one of the cottage walls in Moreton led to the discovery of part of the shaft of the cross. After repair work, the cross was set up and rededicated in Chew Stoke churchyard.

Moreton was closely associated with two other manors to the north of the area, Walley and St Cross, both having families with those names, or variants of them (see below). The ownership of these three manors became linked in the 14th century.

As noted above, after the middle of the 14th century the manor of Moreton passed through several hands. From the excavations that could be carried out in the time available there was no evidence that any of these undertook any building at Moreton and this could have been a contributory factor in its decline in that period.

Documents and early histories tell us who held the manor at various times. Some of these holders of particular local interest are as follows.

One well-known holder in 1379 was Sir Matthew Gournay and Alice his (second) wife. He was the youngest son of the Sir Thomas de Gournay who had held the manor of West Harptree Gournay among several others. Sir Thomas had been implicated as one of the main participants in the murder of Edward II at Berkeley Castle and so had forfeited his estates. Sir Matthew therefore had no inheritance but had acquired a sizeable estate by the time of his death (at the age of 90), as a famous and successful soldier fighting in the wars against France and by three advantageous marriages. He regained royal favour and recovered the manors of West Harptree Gournay and Widcombe (which both later devolved to the Crown and became part of the Duchy of Cornwall estates), as well as being granted others.

In 1428 John Seintlow, or St Loe, held half a knight's fee (the obligation to provide an armed knight to fight in the king's campaigns for a specified number of days each year) in Moreton. The other half of the fee was held by a William Venour. John St Loe was a member of the prominent local family of that name that held manors (e.g. Knighton Sutton) in Chew Magna and gave their name to Newton St Loe.

The manor of 'Mourton Wroughton' appears in a document of 1603 as being in the possession of Jane Still, and is mentioned again in another document following her death on 30 September 1608. This may be taken to refer to Moreton, as an earlier holder in 1515 had been Sir Christopher Wroughton.

Jane Still was the second wife, and then for a few months until her own death, the widow, of John Still, who was the Bishop of Bath and Wells from 1593 until his death in February 1608. She was also the daughter of John Horner of Cloford, the famous 'Little Jack Horner' of the nursery rhyme, who acquired the valuable manor of Mells at the dissolution of the monasteries. From the documents we know that she was the sister of Sir Thomas Horner of Cloford and that she had a son and heir Thomas who was twelve years old at the time of her death. Because the heir was a minor and the manor was held directly from 'the king in chief by knight service', King James I had the potentially lucrative right at that time to the 'wardship' of Thomas. This meant that he was entitled to the proceeds of the estate until the heir came of age and the right to decide whom the heir should marry. An inquisition was therefore held at Yeovil into the assets and their value. These were stated to be 'The manor of Morton alias Mourton Wroughton with appurtenances. One capital messuage and farm in Compton Martin called Mourton Farm and one water mill in Compton Martin belonging to it with appurtenances'. The worth was established after a survey to be £6 13s 4d. It is interesting that at a previous inquisition at Wells it had been initially claimed that the manor and its appurtenances were held 'of John May esquire as of his manor of Blagdon' – harking back to the days of the FitzMartins. The Wells inquisition was probably more sympathetic to retaining the manor under family control and this would of course have deprived the King of his money. However, his officers were clearly on the ball in this case and James I promptly sold the wardship to George Lord Carew for £24 – £12 'in hand' and £12 in eight months time.

The farms and cottages at Moreton existing when the reservoir was built mainly date from the 18th century. The largest of these was Moreton Farm, a rectangular building built of local stone with its outbuildings set round a square yard. Some of this stone would have been salvaged from earlier derelict buildings and a stone in

Moreton Farm

one of the walls had the date 1579. Traces of an earlier building included a large inglenook in the old kitchen with a cross-beam eight foot six inches long and a bread oven. The house had two staircases, one of which led down to the old kitchen, and all the bedrooms led through one another as there was no corridor upstairs.

The story of Joseph Leech and his visit to Moreton Farm in the 1850s described in his 'Rural Rides' is widely known and it was often referred to in articles around the time of the reservoir construction. It is worth repeating briefly here, however, as it provides an eye-witness account of life as it was 150 years ago. Joseph Leech was a journalist and newspaper proprietor, the founder of The Bristol Times. He would attend Sunday services at the various churches around Bristol and describe these, including what he thought of the sermons, in a column under the name of 'The Church Goer'. He used to patronise the stall in Bristol Market of a 'Mistress Jenny K', who sold butter, eggs and pork from her home at Moreton Farm. She was 'of honest face and a portly person' and walked the seven miles to and from market every day. One day, she found out who he was and invited him to visit her for a meal one Sunday after hearing the sermon at a local church – she suggested Compton Martin but he got the time of the service there wrong and went to Chew Stoke instead. He arrived at the farm on his cob John Bunyan, which he took to a stall in the byre and went into the kitchen.

There, seated on a semi-circular high-backed settle by the capacious fireplace with her esteemed and worthy goodman, I found my friend Mistress Jenny K (in her old market beaver bonnet). The back of the settle was turned to the door so I came on them unawares and it was not until I had taken a survey of both and the apartment that they were conscious of my having entered.

There was a fine sea coal and log fire down which blazed and crackled and shed a ruddy lustre on everything around in that cleanly comfortable and well-kept kitchen, making the rows of polished pewter plates on the dresser shine with a brilliancy that beat her Majesty's best silver service; and lighting up a hundred curious culinary articles, in the surface of which you might see yourself, and which hung upon hooks and rested upon shelves round about.

He goes on to say that they had before them on a table a bible and prayer book from which 'the goodman' was reading, while an old setter dog on a mat in the inglenook watched them 'with an almost intelligent affection and interest'.

The census returns for the years 1841 to 1871 show that the occupier of Moreton Farm was John King. In 1881 and 1891 respectively, the occupiers were James Emery and Edward Cole.

It is interesting to note that the 1891 census for Moreton includes Mary Baker, a widow of 64, who describes herself as a market woman, living in one of the cottages; also to compare Mistress Jenny's daily walk with that of Lily Holbrook's mother, at Herons Green Farm, below.

Grove Farm, between the crossroads and the mill, was built in 1737 as indicated by the builder's date stone above the door. As with other buildings of that date it was built of local stone, had a large inglenook, and floors in some of the older bedrooms made from irregular planks cut from tree trunks. It also had a solid oak settle in the kitchen, which the grandfather of the last farmer's wife had reputedly carried from Priddy to the farm on his shoulders. A door had the initials and dates of previous occupiers carved into it.

During the 19th century the census returns tell us that from 1841 to 1871 the occupiers of Grove Farm were the Roynon family. By the 1901 census the head of the household was George Cole.

Information during this period about the other smaller farms in Moreton is sparse. Although photographs were taken of the buildings, there is no description of interesting architectural details or artefacts as was recorded for other buildings. We know that Chestnut Farm would have had a thatched roof because a valuation for a mortgage dated 1 March 1928 says that this is to be replaced by a new tiled roof at a cost of about £70.

Information is also difficult to come by about the occupiers because the census returns do not necessarily name the buildings (and the names sometimes change also). In any case, some farms changed hands frequently and the cottages (usually occupied by agricultural workers) even more frequently.

Because research has been carried out independently into the King family, we know that George King was the occupier of Yewtree Farm from 1881 to 1901; that Kings and Keels were at Chestnut Farm during 1841 to 1901; and that Kings were at Cross (or Laurel) Farm in 1841, 1851 and 1901.

St Cross and the St Cross family

The second medieval site of importance that was excavated was what was known as the St Cross Nunnery. This site was about halfway along a line between Moreton and Woodford House near to Whitehall Farm and was known locally as Nunnery Fields. The lane going a short distance northward from the crossroads at Moreton, called Northfield Lane, may possibly have been part of an original way to this site, though evidence from the excavation throws some doubt on this theory.

The St Cross Nunnery was linked to the family of St Cross (de Sancta Cruce) who held the manor of that name over a similar period to the de Moretons. Tradition had it (based on Collinson's History of Somerset and other publications) that Elizabeth de Sancta Cruce established cells for four nuns on a site near Chew Stoke, which was identified as St Cross on a map of 1762. The excavations did indeed find the remains of a significant number of moated buildings at the identified site, but no evidence to suggest that these buildings contained a nunnery.

It was considered more likely that the buildings were in fact a manor or farmstead belonging to the St Cross family.

The St Cross family also had dealings with the lords of the manor of Harptree, as a letter from Thomas Ap Adam, lord of East Harptree, to his seneschal (steward) Thomas de Gournay in the reign of Edward III shows. He says that his father, John Ap Adam, had made an exchange of enclosed parcels of land in East and West Harptree with Peter de Sancta Cruce and his wife Agnes, and that he wants this land back in his own hands. Perhaps this Peter is the 'Petrus de Santa Cruce' who was assessed for 2s in the 1327 Lay Subsidies under West Harptree.

Walley Court Farm, Chew Stoke

Walley Court, the Le Waleys and Gilbert families

Walley Court was a three storey, L-shaped building of stone rubble with an ashlar façade. The façade dated from the first quarter of the 18th century although the building was older. It is likely that this was the building, occupied by a Mr Adams, which was the first of the three properties in the lake area specifically identified on B Donn's map of eleven miles round Bristol, published in 1769.

Under the house there was a vaulted cellar, and a stone spy hole or ventilation shaft from the cellar was saved and installed in the porch of the church at Chew Stoke. One of the main features of the house was the main staircase that extended to all three floors, and had corkscrew balusters and newel posts richly carved in a rustic style. Over the fireplace in the ground floor room at the back of the house was a large wooden lintel probably dating back to the 15th century. Philip Rahtz considered that this was more likely to have been installed from elsewhere, rather than to have survived in place from an earlier building on the site. However, some re-used painted and carved stones from an earlier building were found beneath the roof at the time of demolition.

Above the entrance porch at Walley Court stood a carved stone effigy of a lady holding an anchor, which is now also in the porch of the church at Chew Stoke. There is a local tradition that this effigy was presented by Queen Elizabeth I to a member of the Gilbert family, who then lived at Walley Court and was one of her sea captains, following the successful defeat of the Spanish Armada. He was also said to have been a relative of Sir Walter Raleigh. If this were so, he would have been Sir Walter's half-brother Sir John Gilbert, who was Vice Admiral in Devon.

Furthermore, the Gilbert at Walley Court was said to have been a descendant of the le Waleys family. This connection between the Gilbert family and the le Waleys family seems to be borne out by a document in the custody of Bridgewater Corporation that settled a dispute that came to court in 1476.

The origin of the dispute was a perpetual chantry founded in the chapel of the Blessed Mary at Woolavington by Gilbert le Waleys, who held land there in the 13th century, with the post of chaplain to be appointed by himself and his heirs. As Gilbert died without children, his heirs were his younger brother Hugh le Waleys and his descendants, who changed their surname to Gilbert over the generations. In 1476 the post of chaplain fell vacant and more than one person claimed the right to appoint the next one. A certain Joan Pym, daughter of Richard Gilbert and wife of Roger Pym, provided the evidence in court to prove her descent from Hugh le Waleys and won the case.

In the latter part of the 19th century the occupiers were farmers, first the Keels and then the Stowells, both local families who were farming in the valley at the construction of the reservoir – the Keels being again at Walley Court.

Woodford House

Woodford Farm is the second of the three buildings marked on B Donn's 1769 map, although it does not state who lived there. It is shown on the opposite side of the river from the Woodford House site, near to the location of Denny Farm. This may just have been a mistake of the map maker so it is probably not worthwhile reading too much into this.

Woodford House, on the site close to where Woodford Mill used to stand, probably dated from the early 19th century. It had rooms with high ceilings and had an unusual ceiling in the dining room formed of heavily moulded wooden squares. It had a dairy, stables, harness room and wood store and fifteen acres of orchard and pasture. A cottage in the grounds occupied the site of a much older building that probably dated from Elizabethan times.

The resident in what was then called 'Woodford Villa' over the period 1861-72 was John Dixon, who was the annatto and mustard maker at Woodford Mill, which would support the proposition that the earlier residents were also the millers. Later on the residents take on an ecclesiastical flavour with the Reverend Edward Clowes, vicar of Bishop Sutton, living there in 1883, and the Reverend George Bowden, the Wesleyan minister at Chew Stoke, living there from 1889-97.

A local tradition in Chew Stoke has it that Jane Austen once paid a visit to Woodford House. Unfortunately, there is no hard evidence for this but it would be nice to think that she did come – perhaps to do some research for a book!

The Denny farms

A site to the south-west of what is now Denny Island and close to Denny House Farm was examined by Philip Rahtz. This proved to include a quarry of a stone found extensively at Moreton and St Cross, which indicated that it might have been in use in medieval times. Also discovered were the foundations of a Georgian house, which is shown on the tithe map (c1839).

References to Denny and Denny House appear just before the 16th century. In 1495 in his will, Thomas Mayoo of Chew directs that 40 shillings each should be paid to Thomas Veale and his sister Agnes, the children of John Veale 'late of Deny'. Several years later on 16 January, 1556, Thomas Vele of Chew, husbandman, made his will. Among other bequests he gave 'To John Veale of Deny haulf and dysen of sylv' spones . . . The cattle at Denye save the too oxen betwixte John Vele and Johan Vele (probably his wife Joan) . . . To John Vele all the woldecorne at Deny all the new corne to John Veale and Johan Veale. The household stuff at Denye to remain in the house.'

Sixteen years later on 16 January 1572, the will of John Veale/Vele of Chew, husbandman (the beneficiary named by Thomas) does not mention Denny. However, on 3 April 1594 in his will, William Fyesher of Chew Magna, yeoman, leaves his wife Elizabeth 'land called Dennye House' – one of his witnesses is another Thomas Veale. Furthermore, one of the witnesses to William's brother George Fisher's will dated 14 May 1598 is 'John Veale of Deny'.

The Hasell family appears in connection with Denny in 1607 in the will of John Hasell of Chew Stoke, when he leaves six acres of land in Denny Marsh to his sons John and William.

From the document dated 1841 about the right of way from Whitehall Farm across the Denny estate to Bishop Sutton (discussed below) we know that there were three owners then of the 'Denny Estate'. They were Mary Poynton (a spinster), the Reverend Francis Poynton, both of Kelston near Bath, and Edward Poynton a merchant of Geelong in 'the Colony of Victoria in Western Australia'.

There were three separate farms with the name of Denny: Denny Farm, near the

River Chew close to Woodford House; Denny House Farm on the hill that is now Denny Island; and what was called in the 1950s Denny 'Hills' Farm, slightly further to the east. The last referred to the Hills family, who occupied the farm then – at the 1901 census it is just called Denny.

According to the date stone above the middle window at the front, which bears the initials 'H F M', Denny Farm was built in 1787. It was said that the Hasell family had occupied the farm continuously since then.

Denny House Farm was probably built in the early 19th century. Its style was plain rather than elegant, with well proportioned rooms and it stood on a site with splendid views. Perhaps this building replaced the Georgian building whose foundations were discovered near the quarry or took its name from there. Many artefacts from this farm were earmarked for the Blaise Castle Museum, including the door and an iron lock.

Denny 'Hills' Farm comprised an original house plus a later extension alongside. It had a massive nail-studded front door, an inglenook with a vast hearth, a double staircase, many corridors and several bedrooms. An outstanding feature was the two magnificent cedars of Lebanon that stood outside and which had been planted in about 1770, perhaps not long after the original house was built. The wood from these was used in the construction of the original Woodford Lodge. An interesting mechanism was found when the chimney breast was demolished. This was thought to have been connected to a roasting jack and possibly driven by wind in some way. This artefact is now held by the Blaise Castle Museum.

Whitehall Farm, Chew Stoke c1950

Whitehall Farm

Whitehall Farm can be traced back to at least 1708, the back of the building having been the oldest part while the front of the building dated from about 1850 or so. This may have had something to do with the change in access to the highway from the farm that is described later on in connection with the turnpike roads.

In 1788 the property was held by the Symes. Documents relating to their title to ownership, on which a legal opinion was needed at that time, tell us who the owners and occupiers were from 1700 up to that date; who provided the mortgages to fund the purchases; and who acted in other capacities. The full story can be seen in Appendix A.

There were six owners of the property over the period. The extent of the property mentioned in the documents varied over time but typically comprised buildings and about 31 acres of land. The story starts when William Webb of Chew Stoke took out a 99 year lease in 1700. His daughter Mary and her husband Richard Heale of Chew Stoke owned the property from 1714 until 1728 when they sold it to John Lukins also of Chew Stoke. John Lukins married Judith and they occupied the property for 25 years until 1753 when they settled it on their daughter Mary and her future husband, John Plaister of Wrington.

The Plaisters probably did not occupy the property as the following year John Plaister sold it to their tenant James Dando of Chew Stoke. Fifteen years later in 1769 James Dando settles a dwelling house, garden, orchard, outbuildings and arable land on his daughter Mary Symes and her husband Samuel Symes of Bristol, who by 1771 were holding the property on a mortgage of £500 from Tobias Peters of Chew Stoke. It is the continuing existence of this mortgage until 1787, through the deaths of Tobias and of both his executors, that seems to have been the trigger for needing a legal opinion.

An interesting pair of characters to appear on the scene are Dr Claver Morris and Richard Comes of Wells, who acted as trustees for the sale of manorial rights in the property to Richard Heale in 1718. Claver Morris was the diarist who is buried in Wells Cathedral – an extract from his diary is in the entrance to Wells Library. Mr Comes appears in his diary as an associate in connection with official business. He may well have been a lawyer.

James Walker, father of the well-known local journalist Eldred Walker, was the tenant of Whitehall Farm in 1861. In 1874 he wanted to construct a new dairy and approached the then owner, a clergyman in Leicestershire, for permission to do so, which was refused for some reason. Nonetheless, he went ahead himself and had the dairy built by a local builder. When the owner learned about this he was enraged and terminated the tenancy straight away.

Chew Park Farm and Chew Park House

Chew Park Farm was the site of the Roman villa but evidence was also found of medieval lime kilns. It was concluded that the stones from the Roman villa would have provided the raw material. The lime produced would either have been used to spread on the fields or for the mortar used in the construction of the churches in the area, which was occurring at that time.

Chew Park Farm (called Chew Park, as the later building of Chew Park House nearby did not then exist) was the third of the properties in the lake area

The Lyons family, Reginald, Norah, Jane Ann, John, Leslie, Chew Park Farm 1928

specifically identified on B Donn's 1769 map. The occupier was named as 'Brichdale Esquire' – perhaps a subtle social distinction between him and the 'Mr Adams' occupying Walley Court?

The building was said to be of the 17th century, with stone mullioned windows, large beams, wide floorboards and nail-studded doors. A particularly interesting piece of furniture was a large upstairs cupboard having a wide board holding pegs with a semi-circular piece of wood fastened to each. The purpose of this cupboard provides an interesting insight into an aspect of local life. It was suggested that during winter, snowbound visitors would spend the night sleeping in the corridors and would use this as a communal cupboard. Several of the artefacts from here were earmarked for the Bristol City Museum.

The will of James King of Moreton, proved at Wells in March 1854, mentions his son John, and John's sons John Henry and James, who is referred to as 'of Chew Park'. This may have been the John King who was mentioned in an abstract of title to Grove Farm made in 1917. This title refers to the wills of John King, late of Chew Park, yeoman, who died on 25 August 1858, and of Sarah King, widow, of Chew Park, who died on 28 November 1895. Perhaps John King is also the Mr John King, yeoman, to whom Robert Blinman Dowling conveyed, on 9 April 1845, two closes of arable land (one called Chew Park of about one acre) 'situated at Bishop Sutton in the parish of Chew Magna'.

Chew Park House was a more recent building, apparently having been built at the turn of the 19th century. By the census of 1901, Chew Park House has been built and is occupied by John H King, a farmer aged 57, and his family – probably John Henry King, the son of the John King mentioned above.

Spring Farm, Mead Farm and Herons Green Farm

Spring Farm and Mead Farm were near each other at Sutton Wick. Spring Farm dated from early in the 16th century and the architectural features of the house indicated that it was built originally as a much grander place than a farmhouse. These features included the heavy nail-studded door, iron window fittings and mullioned frames, and a huge Tudor chimney-piece in the kitchen. A great barn, 67 feet long 33 feet wide and 35 feet to the apex of the roof stood beside the farmhouse. As the manor was originally held by the Bishop of Bath and Wells, it was considered that in medieval times it could have been used by the bishops themselves or as the home of the bailiff of the estate.

The Baber family occupied the farm in the 19th century and it was said that Edward Baber, one of seven sons, had a party trick in which he used to jump over a five-barred gate while holding a half-gallon jar of cider in each hand.

Mead Farm was also thought to have been originally the site of a much grander building. Apart from the general surroundings of sprawling outbuildings, however, the only evidence for this was the large inglenook with a gigantic carved oak beam

Spring Farm built in the early 16th century

nine foot long, similar to that removed from Walley Court. The theory was that the inglenook alone had survived the destruction of the previous building and that the modest replacement building had been constructed round it.

Herons Green Farm (not the farm close by now bearing that name) was described in the mid 1950s as a modern building, which appeared to have replaced an earlier thatched one. The kitchen of the previous building, with its large inglenook and fine oak framing and spacious window-seat had been kept in use as a store room.

The occupiers in the 19th century included William King and from 1876 Henry Maggs, whose daughter Lily, later Mrs Holbrook, held the tenancy until the reservoir was built. The description of her mother's daily routine, as told to and recorded by Mr F C Jones of BWW, bears comparison with the story of Jenny the market woman of Moreton Farm, mentioned earlier.

> *She would rise at five am, scald the milk, make the cream, cook breakfast for the family and farm labourers, dress the baby, and unattended walk from Compton Martin over Dundry carrying the baby with her. Business transacted, without bite or drink she would walk back to Herons Green Farm still carrying the baby. Then began her real day's work – milking the cows, driving the horses, cutting the hay, working in dairy or piggery.*

Her mother lived to be 90 and Mrs Holbrook had a photograph of her father ploughing a field at the age of 84.

A one year lease dated 1714 by Simon Norris of Chew Stoke, yeoman, to Joseph Lane of Chew Stoke, stocking maker, may possibly refer to the previous building on the site. The lease concerns a 'messuage and land at Heron's Green (Herring's Green), a former house but now converted into a barn called Saunder's barn, and a house called the Dye house'. It seems to suggest that the present name may be a corruption of a previous one, regardless of the presence of nesting herons in 1955. Could this Joseph Lane be the person of the same name that provided the £120 for Richard Heale to buy Whitehall Farm in 1718?

Highways and lanes

The coming of the turnpike roads will have made great improvements to the highways to the west and south of the lake area. The Bristol Turnpike Trust's Bristol to Wells turnpike via Dundry passed through Chew Stoke (where Turnpike Cottage marks the original toll house) to the Blue Bowl and then by-passed West Harptree to the west by a new road over the Mendips. The Trust's parish boundary marker between West Harptree and Compton Martin parishes still stands by the wall of the White Cottage near the Blue Bowl.

One direct effect of the building of this turnpike can be seen from documents relating to Whitehall Farm. When Charles Ransford Court of Wrington bought Whitehall Farm at auction in 1841, a plan of the property based on the Tithe Commutation Act of 1840 shows a road from the turnpike to the house (passing initially through land belonging to a Mr Colthurst). The map also shows a field gate at the eastern boundary of the property marked 'To Sutton'.

A second document dated 13 June 1861 explains this gate. This document is a release of a right of way, except as a footpath only, by the same Charles Ransford Court (now of Cotham Bristol) owner of 'an estate called Whitehall now in the occupation of James Walker' to the owners of 'an estate called The Denny'. The document states that the owners and occupiers of Whitehall Farm 'have for a long period had a right of way as well as for carts carriages implements of husbandry horses sheep and cattle as for persons on foot over the said close of pasture land called Pennsylvania and Plain Field to a messuage and farm buildings upon the said estate called Whitehall from the highway leading from Woodford Mill to Chew Stoke'. The owners of 'The Denny' paid £70 to have this right of way across their land cancelled so it must have been a valuable asset for Whitehall Farm in its day.

It seems that the longer journey via the turnpike road was a much better route to Bishop Sutton for vehicles and stock than the old more direct way via Woodford – although the latter was still quicker on foot.

The West Harptree Turnpike Trust was a much smaller organisation, whose main toll road – following basically the line of the present A368 – ran between Marksbury (where it joined the Bath to Wells turnpike) and Churchill (where it met the Bristol to Bridgewater turnpike). It cut a new route through the complex of lanes in the Bishop Sutton area and provided a much improved road for wagons carrying coal from the Bishop Sutton mines to the lead processing works on Mendip. The Trust also provided links from Chew Magna to the other main turnpike roads.

Most of the original lanes were stopped up during the construction of the reservoir and it is natural to assume that this was the case for each of the lanes round the lake that now come to a dead end. This was not the case for Stitchings Shord Lane near Bishop Sutton, however, which is shown on the 1904 OS map as continuing as a field track for a short distance after passing Stitchings Shord Farm. In earlier times, according to the tithe map of c1839, this track then turned sharply right along a field boundary to stop again in an area of fields identified as marshy ground and directly in line with a short extension of Stratford Lane called Marshley Lane. Perhaps these two lanes did at some time in the past meet and provide a way from the Moreton area to Bishop Sutton, although the through roads shown here on the David and Charles reprint of the first edition of the one inch Ordnance Survey map must surely be dubious.

The 1901 census returns

The changes between consecutive censuses can sometimes throw a light on social events of the time especially when added to by personal memories. An interesting example from the 1891 and 1901 census returns is worth mentioning. In 1891 at North Widcombe we find the family of George and Emma Cole. Their eldest daughter, Ellen aged nineteen, is a teacher at a National School (she taught at West Harptree). Another daughter, Clara aged eight, is at school as is her brother, Frederick aged seven. There are two more sons and two daughters with ages ranging from fifteen to four. At Herriotts Mill live Rosina Baker a widow and her son George aged 23.

Ten years later, in 1901, Ellen Cole is now Mrs Ellen Baker and living at Herriotts Mill with her husband George and their young family of four sons ranging from one to six years old. Clara is now married to Leonard Maggs living at Moreton and with a daughter aged one. Frederick Cole is now working for the Hassells at Stratford Mill as a corn miller. George, Emma and the rest of the family have also moved to Moreton where George is now a farmer on his own account having ten years previously worked as an agricultural labourer.

The 1901 census provides a snapshot of who was living in the area at the turn of the 19th century, including the families, servants and others resident on the day of the census. It therefore provides an appropriate close to this period and an opening to the period when personal memories come into play. The details of those living in the houses affected by the reservoir scheme are included in Appendix B.

CHAPTER FOUR

Mills and Early Water Extraction

Today the River Chew, as visible at Litton or Shrowle before entering the lake, is but a shadow of its former size. In 1846 the newly formed Bristol Waterworks Company started to extract water from the river to meet the demands of the growing city of Bristol. This was to change the river forever and contribute to the gradual decline in the numerous businesses that had used these waters for centuries to turn their mill-wheels. Before we look at how and when the river water was extracted, let us study the variety and location of the mills on the Chew. They illustrate the range of rural industries, which were eventually to be put out of business by the rapid development of machinery and the growth of large factory mills during the industrial revolution.

Milling in the upper Chew Valley

For hundreds of years the waters of the Chew helped to quench the thirst of our ancestors and their animals. They also provided the means to drive the grinding stones in the numerous watermills that sprang up alongside the river and its tributaries. There were at various times up to 40 mills along its seventeen miles, although it should be said that these operations varied greatly in size. Some were well established commercial businesses built on a particularly good stretch of the river, whilst others were small, one-man operations, near a convenient spring.

Not only were the mills of varying sizes, they also had a number of different uses during their lifetimes. Some made paper or were used in the cloth industry. Some ground logs, others were snuff mills; at least one made gunpowder, another mustard and many were grist (corn) mills.

Perhaps not surprisingly, records of these rural enterprises are not plentiful. In some cases just a single note in a will or a parish record is all there is to tell us that some of these places existed at all. Thankfully those who compiled the Domesday Survey (1086) left a comprehensive record and note that there were over five and a half thousand mills across the country.

Chewton Mendip to Shrowle

The Domesday Survey for Somerset records that there were five mills at Chewton Mendip with a total value of 30 shillings less five pennies. Yet today there is little, if any, physical evidence in the village of their size or location.

There was certainly a corn mill about half a mile further along the road at Litton. It was offered for sale in 1812 as 'A capital and well-accustomed new built water grist mill, well supplied with water, working two pair of excellent french stones; together with a new built dwelling house and a small garden'. In the early 1920s the site of this mill was built over when the main road was diverted to the south of the village. It is thought that there was another mill further in the village near the church.

There were two mills in close proximity to each other at nearby Sherborne where a powerful spring rose to combine with the Chew. The older lower mill was probably a fulling mill until the early 1800s, and this is evidenced in the tithe map c1839 which names two nearby fields as 'Rack Close'. Fulling was one of the last stages of cloth production. It involved pounding the newly woven fabric with large stones in a pit filled with water and fuller's earth. This helped the fibres to thicken and bond together. Racks were the wooden constructions erected near to mills on which the wet broadcloths or medleys were stretched and hung out to dry on 'tenterhooks'. (Medleys or 'Spanish cloths' were made by mixing wool treated with various dyes prior to spinning to create a range of different colours.) The cloth industry had for some years been moving away from the Chew area in favour of Frome and Bradford on Avon and by 1840 the lower mill had been converted to a grist mill and was grinding cereals for low grade flour and for animal feed. It was still doing this in 1883 when Sarah Banwell, the owner, accepted £300 as compensation for loss of water supply from BWW who were about to tap the previously plentiful spring and lay a new pipeline into the city.

The nearby upper mill was at one time making paper. It was one of a number of small concerns in North Somerset that concentrated on paper manufacture. Many went out of business in the early part of the 19th century, as they were unable to invest in more modern machinery. Some evidence of the problems in the industry can be found in the parish records for nearby Compton Martin which, in 1821, speak of 'papermakers in distress'. The Compton Martin mill, which stood where the pond is, ceased working around 1830.

Sherborne upper mill had itself also stopped paper manufacture by 1850, by which time a gentleman by the name of Elisha Tucker was operating there as a Button Dealer. The buttons were made from animal horns and local people used to tell of the women who would walk right across the Mendips to Cheddar where they collected newly made, part finished shirts that they brought back over 'the top' to have button holes made and buttons attached. The finished bundles were then carried all the way back to Cheddar and a fresh lot collected. How long the business continued to operate is not clear but the buildings were certainly no longer in use in 1885 when the new pipeline was laid.

The tiny hamlet of Coley seemingly had two mills. The grist mill on the road up to Hinton Blewett is well known. However, when John Collinson published his 'History & Antiquities of Somerset' in 1791, he also mentioned a fulling mill there but its location is not known today. The grist mill was for many years a successful business and many local housewives thought that the flour ground there made excellent bread.

A local farmer remembered Coley Mill when he was a young boy:

My father always grew corn at Widcombe and we grew quite a bit of barley. He'd take it to the mills and get it ground. I used to come along to Coley Mill when it was running. Bobby Masters owned it. John Small was my father's carter. He drove the horses and cart and he'd put up seven or eight bags of corn, perhaps two hundredweight in a sack and I'd sit up in the front quietly and ride along with him and see all that's going on. I'd watch Austin Wookey take the bag, put the chain on, pull a lever, and take the bag up in the top of the mill.

Austin Wookey who worked at the mill became something of a local celebrity with his stories of rural life on the Mendips. The miller, Bobby Masters, died in 1930 and the mill was pulled down shortly after.

Shrowle had a corn mill until the early 19th century although at one time it may possibly have been a fulling mill as a field in the hamlet is named 'Rack Close' on the tithe map of c1839. A stream diverted off the river close to Tudor Farm probably supplied the mill.

Herriotts Mill

A few hundred yards further on stood Herriotts Mill at North Widcombe, in the parish of West Harptree. It was certainly a corn mill for at least 500 years as a grant of 1426 stated that 'tenants of West Harptree and Wydecombe shall always grind at this mill'. However, by the end of the 18th century it was being used for other purposes and was in need of updating. In 1805, an article in the Bristol Mirror mentioned the offer for sale of 'A capital mill with a small tenement, garden, orchard, and paddock. – The premises are now in order (a large sum of

Herriotts Mill c1900

money having lately been expended on them in additional building and repairs) and well adapted for a leather dresser, clothier or papermaker'. The mill was indeed being used to produce paper in 1816 when Charles Gunn was in charge at Herriotts, but the changes in that industry meant that by 1830 the mill had reverted to grinding corn. For the next 100 years or so just two families occupied the premises. William Sweetland and his wife (later widow), Sarah, ran the business until the 1860s after which the Baker family took over. John Baker had run the nearby Stratford Mill and the Crown Inn, at West Harptree, for a time before moving to Herriotts. His son George Weaver Baker was still the miller at the time of the 1901 census.

By the 1930s the buildings were derelict, like so many in the area that would eventually disappear beneath the new lake. The end came when the Bishop Sutton to West Harptree road was diverted to run where the mill once stood. Today, people park nearby to relax, eat countless ice creams and admire the wildlife.

Herriotts was the first of four mills that were to be submerged during the formation of Chew Valley Lake.

Woodford Mill

The mill of which we know least is Woodford Mill near Chew Stoke. It was probably a fulling mill during the 16th and 17th century when the cloth industry was flourishing in the area to the south of Bristol. It was certainly a flour mill in 1839 when a James Mills owned it. Two years later it was put up for auction as 'All that substantial well built grist mill and a close of rich meadow land on the River Chew, driving three pairs of stones'. Business was obviously good at the time as the mill was also 'well supplied with grist from the surrounding neighbourhood' and there was also 'an exclusive right of fishery, which is notorious for its excellent trout'.

The continuing changes in use can be seen twenty years later when the mill was now in the possession of John Dixon, an annatto and mustard maker. Annatto was an orange-red dye obtained by crushing the pulp from the fruit of the annabatta tree from Central America. It was used amongst other things for colouring cheese. By 1866 the business was under the control of George Arter at his 'West of England Annatto Works, Woodford Mills, Chew Stoke'. Arter ran a similar operation not far away at the mill in Stowey Bottom. Manufacture ceased by the 1880s when a process was introduced at Winford using red ochre from nearby Regil.

Moreton Mill

The ancient hamlet of Moreton was home to another mill that would one day end up under the lake. The site was occupied from at least the 12th century and there were two or three separate phases of building. Philip Rahtz dated the mill house from the late 16th century and thought that possibly the last mill to be built dated from that period also. The mill house was surrounded by a large moat that helped to keep the area inside dry during the frequent floods. At one stage, it also had three large ovens, possibly used by the miller to bake bread for the neighbourhood.

Although a corn mill for most of its life, Moreton did have a different use in the late 18th century. It had been decided, following many accidents, that the making of gunpowder should be moved away from areas of high population, such as Bristol, to rural areas. This was to prove unfortunate for Thomas Urch who died in 1799 'in consequence of having been burnt in a most dreadful manner at the powder mills'. Joseph Gaskell was to suffer a similar fate when he 'was blown to pieces through standing too close to the fire with gunpowder in his pocket'!

By 1861, the mill was again grinding corn and did so until the start of the 1900s when it ceased operating. Although two cottages remained in use, the mill building fell into disrepair. By 1954, when the BWW contractors moved in to start preparing the site, it was derelict.

Rusty machinery lay unwanted. A path made of old broken millstones was long since unused, and clumps of nettles and wild primroses had taken over the gardens. Ivy covered the collapsed walls. The sluice gate, over which the foaming water used to rush, was still intact although the stream was now covered with water mint.

Stratford Mill

The other mill site to be ultimately flooded and the only one still in working condition up until the 1950s was Stratford Mill in West Harptree. This is the mill for which we have the most documentary records. In addition we were fortunate to interview two of the daughters of Arthur Wilson who was the last miller. They spent their childhood in the house attached to the mill and shared with us some of their memories. The overwhelming feeling that comes across when listening to them is that of a wonderfully happy childhood in a peaceful rural haven.

> *It was a great old place and such an idyllic situation with the pond and the river. Lovely – and always something going on.*
>
> *We had a beautiful house. It was to the right of the mill. There were four bedrooms with a little annex down in, like we used to call a little box room. It was very primitive, you know at Stratford but the house was in very good condition. It wasn't damp and Mother always had a lovely fire. But I didn't care for the winters; it was very, very cold. There was no running water and no electric light. It was all candles and in the kitchen we had to pump the water up from outside.*

There was a mill of one sort or other at Stratford for centuries. On many sites along the Chew, old worn out buildings were often substantially altered or even demolished and a new mill built close by. Stratford was no exception. It was situated alongside the Roman road that led up onto the Mendips. The Domesday Survey (1086) mentions a mill in West Harptree which was almost certainly at Stratford, and in the 1327 Lay Subsidy roll, Walterus de Stratforde was assessed at two shillings for the mill.

The last mill to be constructed on the site began operating towards the end of the 18th century. It was a three-storey building with thick stone walls and massive roof trusses, 'built like a fort'. The machinery, mostly made of apple-wood, was said to turn with a smoothness not found in iron or steel. But it was not just a mill it was also a small farm and, as records show, for many families over the years, it was very much a home.

When she made her will in 1789, Sarah Dowling left her nephew, William Andrews, 'all that part of a messuage or tenement in West Harptree called Stratford Mill which I purchased of Benjamin Collins'. Sarah was obviously quite well off as she also left another property in Harptree together with her clothes, furniture, and over £450 in cash bequests spread amongst a large family. The executors of the will were the same William Andrews and Sarah's grandson, John Collins.

Seven years later John Collins was shown in the parish records, as the owner-occupier of 16 acres of land at the mill with a rateable value of 1d per acre. John died in 1823 and was buried in the churchyard at West Harptree. He willed that his wife, Ann, would take over the mill and that another John, the eldest of his four sons, would rent it from her. The Collins family's occupation of the mill appears to have come to an end in 1828 when Jacob Collins, John senior's brother, who was now the owner, left to take over a nearby farm. In the 1840s and 50s the house was home to John and Rosina Baker and their eight children, but they had moved to take over the 'Crown' in the village by 1855 and Alfred Wookey was now the miller.

It was in 1861 that the young newly-weds Joseph and Ellen Hassell, moved into Stratford Mill. They were originally tenants but by 1865 they had become owners and the mill, which was apparently always kept 'prim and proper', was to stay in the family for the next 65 years. Joseph and Ellen had fifteen children, twelve of whom survived into adulthood.

Joseph and Ellen had both died by 1893 and the relatively young family had to decide who would run the mill. It was their daughter, Florence, who was already caring for her two-year-old brother Percy, who took on the job. Initially, some of her brothers helped her, for in the 1901 census when she is 34, her brothers Arthur then aged 21 and Maurice aged 19 are both described as 'Corn miller, employer'.

When war broke out in 1914, Percy 'answered the call' and joined the Navy, leaving his sister to work on with the help of a miller and a driver. At this time, Gournay Court in West Harptree was used as a hospital for men severely wounded in the conflict. Many of these chaps were pleased to walk or be taken by cart up the narrow lane to the mill for tea parties which Florence, despite the demands of running the business alone, was happy to host. In 1918, Percy himself returned injured and sadly died soon after.

With her other brothers and sisters all long since married and moved away, and the wounded soldiers having returned to their own homes, the house was now a much quieter place. But it was still home for Florence and she carried on running the business until her death in 1930 when the mill was sold to the Duchy of Cornwall.

Nine years later the property was sold on to BWW as part of the preparation for flooding the Chew Valley. Because of its impending fate, the mill was not used and became neglected. However, the outbreak of WW2 meant that work on the reservoir did not go ahead as planned. It was also, a couple of years later, to give the mill an opportunity to work once again.

On the 6 December 1941, Bristol was heavily bombed and the premises of the millers Vowls & Handcock Ltd. were destroyed. A replacement mill was needed and a few weeks later the company agreed a temporary tenancy deal for Stratford Mill with BWW.

The Wilson family was already living in the mill house at this time and was destined to be the last tenants. Arthur Wilson ran the farm with his wife, Harriet, and three daughters, and when Vowls & Handcock took over he started working for them as well. He was an active man who ground corn for himself and some of the local farmers, as well as having a milk round and keeping a dairy herd. He owned pigs and two prize winning Shirehorses and his yard was also home to

Stratford Mill and house from rear (mill on left of main building)

numerous hens and a wonderful flock of geese. He grew apples for his own cider and, in his spare time, was the organist and choirmaster at West Harptree Church!

> *At the back there was steps up through and into the fields beyond where we kept the horses and the hens. There was the milking sheds and there was the stables which was back over. And Mum had a little back garden but it was a very damp garden. It was also very stony and lots of wild flowers used to grow in there.*
>
> *Where the mill-wheel was, you had like an island there, and there was a bridge and you could go over this little bridge and up to the piggery. And then the stream would run straight down to the sides of the orchards each side of us.*
>
> *It was a beautiful place. Big drive with another little bridge, then down to the bottom and out into the lane, which had a big white gate at the bottom.*
>
> *It wasn't Dad's own farm. He had a bit of land but it wasn't a huge lot. I suppose about seven fields and I suppose we had about 30 cattle and there was all that poultry and the two Shirehorses. He won the cup at the Bath & West. For two years he won the cup and he would have had it the third year but they put in a Clydesdale and so he didn't get a look in.*

The cogging and mill-wheel were still in good order but some repair work and additional machinery was installed along with new millstones. For the next four years, the mill took in much of the extra corn produced by local farmers for animal feed and whilst it was often possible to see bombers heading for Bristol and watch searchlights seeking them out at night, it continued working away untouched in its peaceful surroundings. Lorries would arrive daily at the mill and reverse under the canopy from where the sacks of corn were hoisted up to the top floor and emptied into the old wooden grain bins in preparation for grinding.

It had a big area where the lorries used to back in to pick up the grain all ground at the mill, wheat and barley and that. It ran about twice or three times a week. It was very dusty in there and a bit noisy. Dad would never allow us to stay in there, we just watched from a distance.

But with all that water around there was a risk each winter of flooding.

We were only about 20 to 25 feet from the river, not far. I wouldn't say it flooded every winter but when it did it used to come up to the doorstep. Luckily it never came into the house because there were two steps before you came in the back door. But we were all surrounded with water. It was quite exciting actually. It used to last two or three days sometimes and then we had to stay home from school because we couldn't get out.

I remember once when the river was in flood there used to be a little bridge going over to the orchards on the other side of the pond and it was all covered in foam and my sister Brenda stepped on it and disappeared from sight! But she had the presence of mind to hold her hands up and I pulled her out. That was frightening because the river then was so fast.

When the War ended Vowls & Handcock bought the mill at Chew Magna and moved out of Stratford. Arthur Wilson and his family stayed on until 1951 but finally had to leave as work on the reservoir was now well under way. In that last year Arthur took his best ever crop of hay and was heard to say, 'What a pity to think of all this good land under fathoms of water'.

In 1950 BWW arranged with the City Council for the mill to be eventually moved up to Hazel Brook in the grounds of Blaise Castle Folk Museum as a public exhibit. The building and machinery were dismantled in 1952 to be transported piece by piece and then rebuilt over the next two years. Lord Dulverton donated £4000 towards the total cost of £4650 19s 6d needed for the operation. Representatives of the Hassell and Wilson families were at the opening ceremony. The lovely old mill building, which had provided a living for so many hard working families, was saved from the waters of the very river that for centuries gave it life.

Early extraction of water

There are few, if any, large towns in England in which the supply of water is so inadequate as in Bristol.

Such were the findings of a government commission set up in 1840 to look at conditions in large towns and cities. But this had not always been the case. For many centuries the people of Bristol could find ample supplies of fresh water via local springs and wells. Many of these wells were on church or monastic lands and had often been developed using money from rich benefactors, possibly seeking preferential treatment in the afterlife.

In medieval times the more affluent areas also devised their own schemes for further supplying their citizens, using various systems of wooden tanks and lead pipes. This was often supplemented, especially in times of drought, by the 'leders'. The leders or ledermen carried large wooden pails strung across their shoulders on yokes, in the same way as dairymaids. They would often walk miles to a clean source of water and haul it back for a penny or two.

However, the population of England was steadily increasing and from the second half of the 18th century many families were enticed away from the country into the towns and cities in search of work. The industrial revolution was in its infancy and Bristol was an important port with increasing trade with Africa, America and the West Indies. The city soon became crowded. For most people fresh water became harder to find and sanitary arrangements were woefully inadequate. In fact, the Avon and the Frome, the two main rivers through the centre of the city became not much better than open sewers. It was clear that something needed to be done to find new sources of fresh water – fast.

Various schemes were put forward but the only one to offer a supply for the whole city, rather than for selected areas, was that proposed by the newly formed Bristol Waterworks Company. Their plan received the approval of Parliament in July 1846 and they set about fulfilling their pledge to provide fresh drinking water to more than 125,000 citizens.

The supply was to come from three sources well outside the city. One was about five miles away near the village of Barrow Gurney whilst the other two were to be found much further away on the lower slopes of the Mendip Hills. The first to become operational was the Cold Bath Spring at Barrow and water from here began running into Bristol in October 1847. The second supply was to be taken from the River Chew near its source at Chewton Mendip and this was to be joined with the combined outflows from nearby Watery Combe in the hamlet of Ford and Garrow Spring at the top of Harptree Combe.

A condition of the assent for the 1846 bill was that none of the homes, farms, or businesses along its course was to suffer by the diversion of water from the Chew.

To achieve this the river was separated close to the source and part of it, after satisfying the needs of the locals at Chewton, was allowed to follow its original course via three new reservoirs, two at nearby Litton and one further down at Chew Magna on the Winford Brook. These compensation reservoirs impounded water during wet weather and released it during dry spells so that the supply of water in the river could be maintained at a statutory flow of one million gallons per day. This would allow a constant flow to the water driven mills, still in operation, along the river on its route towards Keynsham where it joins the River Avon.

The remaining water then started a journey of more than ten miles, mainly by gravity, to Number 1 reservoir at Barrow Gurney. The route was known as the 'Line of Works' and for its time was certainly a remarkable feat of engineering. The water is directed into a tunnel that heads towards Harptree Combe, collecting the offerings from numerous other springs via inlet pipes along the way. By the time it reaches Proud Cross Farm it is 90 ft below ground. Further on in the eastern arm of Harptree Combe the water is joined by the last of the subsidiary feeders – the outflow of the Garrow Spring.

The conduit emerges in Harptree Combe where it can be seen as an aqueduct raised up on masonry piers. The water then goes back underground further down the Combe before heading past West Harptree and on up to Breach Hill. There, near the junction with Kingshill Lane, a stone obelisk marks the route. The obelisk itself is at the top of a pressure release pipe that allows air and water to escape. The water then emerges again travelling through aqueducts at Leigh and later at Winford before reaching its final destination.

The conduit along the 'Line of Works' is still in use more than 150 years after construction, and the springs at Chewton, and Harptree continue to provide in excess of 3 million gallons of water per day.

Throughout the second half of the 19th century, by a succession of Acts, further powers were granted to BWW by Parliament for the construction of works. Water mains were extended into many suburban areas creating even more demand. In 1884 BWW purchased Sherborne Spring. This water was conveyed by another pipeline for over 13 miles, to gravitate into the covered reservoir at Knowle. The spring had originally driven the waterwheel of lower Sherborne Mill before flowing into the Chew. BWW therefore purchased Sherborne Mill, which ceased operation, and negotiated a financial settlement with the nine remaining mill owners along the river, to compensate them for the reduced flow.

In 1889, to meet the increasing demand for water, BWW constructed a dam across the Yeo valley and impounded the water of the river to create what is now known as Blagdon Lake. This water was then pumped directly to Barrow.

The work at Blagdon, which was completed in 1901, set a precedent for the approach taken in its landscaping and use. BWW endeavoured 'to preserve and enhance the beauty of the countryside' by landscaping and extensive tree planting. Fishing was introduced in 1904 and BWW set up and maintained a trout hatchery at Ubley for restocking the lake. All these features were to be developed at the future Chew Valley Lake.

BWW continued to expand to provide for the ever-increasing demands for water until, in the 1930s, their story once more overlaps with ours. The details of how the water from the River Chew is further tapped to augment public supplies are covered in Chapter 12.

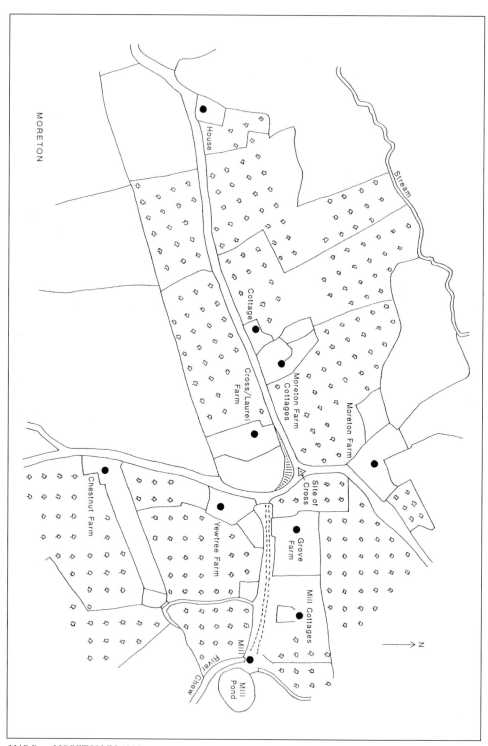

MAP D   *MORETON IN 1938*

CHAPTER FIVE

A Walk Round Moreton in 1938

The hamlet of Moreton lay in the south-western part of the area now covered by the lake. All its buildings were demolished and the sites of almost every single one of these now lie under the water, just off what is shown on the current OS map (1:25,000 scale) as Moreton Point. This map also shows much of what was the original network of lanes to the south of Moreton down to Stratford Lane. These had changed little between the Day & Masters map of 1782, and the map prepared in 1938 by BWW, to show the land expected to be acquired for the reservoir and its associated works. From a schedule prepared at the same time, we know who occupied and farmed the land at Moreton in 1938, and who the owners were as well (see Appendix B). The layout of Moreton is shown in the accompanying sketch map.

What is not shown on the current OS map is the lane to Moreton from the original Chew Stoke to West Harptree road. When the reservoir was built, the main road as it is now was realigned (over the subsidiary dam at Herons Green) from below the lane to Moreton up to Stoke Villice. The line of the previous road (built originally as the turnpike road) was to the east of the present main road – much of it under the lake.

To reach Moreton from the West Harptree direction, passing the Blue Bowl, you would carry on towards Chew Stoke for nearly a mile, almost as far as Ben Bridge, which can still be seen, from the viewpoint at Herons Green Bay, at times of drought when the water level is low. The start of the lane to Moreton formed a triangle, with the field boundaries set back, on the right hand side just before the milestone showing nine miles to Bristol and ten miles to Wells. Eye-witness accounts in later years talk of the 'substantial stone and tile cottages, with their gay flower gardens, comfortable-looking farmhouses and rutted lanes', the lanes bordered by high trees and hedges festooned with honeysuckle and dog roses and of the many raised enclosures marking the sites of medieval dwellings.

The lane sloped gradually downwards towards the centre of the hamlet about half a mile away. The first house on the left, with garden, orchard and stables (the modern BWW cottage is roughly on the same site) was lived in by Arthur and Mrs Derrick in 1938. It was known as Moreton House and was owned by Arthur Perry and Denis Hayward. In the 1950s it was also referred to as Tibbs Cottage, after the last family that occupied it. Arthur Derrick farmed a block of land on the other side of Moreton lying between Moreton Lane, Stratford Lane and the river, and belonging to the same owners.

'You would walk on down through the tall trees here, past the marshes either side.' The lane continued with orchards on either side. Next on the left came three cottages, a single and a pair of semi-detached ones, each with its own front garden. In 1938, Mary Marshall occupied the first cottage, which was owned by Sarah Keel. The next two were Moreton Farm cottages, only one of which appeared to be occupied – by William Powell – at the time of the 1938 schedule.

Next on the right, just before reaching the centre, was Cross Farm (sometimes known as Laurel Farm) where Edgar and Mrs Sims were the owner occupiers. Their land mostly lay close to the farmhouse.

At the centre you came to an offset crossroads with a small green where Moreton Cross used to stand – by this time only the base remained in place. From here, lanes went north (Northfield Lane) and south (Moreton Lane). Just round the corner of Moreton Lane a track went off to the left. Northfield Lane would take you up a short rise to Moreton Farm on the left, where George Curry, the tenant farmer, lived with his family. Moreton Farm (owned, together with the Moreton Farm cottages by Ashton Hunt) was by far the largest in the hamlet at around 230 acres, with the bulk of its land to the north.

The lane past Moreton Farm continued for a short distance between the fields before petering out. However, in earlier times, on the maps of both Day & Masters in 1782 and Greenwood in 1822, this lane is shown as continuing in a curve to the west and meeting the Chew Stoke to West Harptree road. It must have had some purpose then, that was no longer needed.

The rutted cart track off Moreton Lane led down towards Moreton Mill and the River Chew about two hundred yards away. First on the left, down the slope and behind a large front garden, was Grove Farm, another small farm whose tenant was Lewis Cole. This slope was handy in later years to bump start the car at Grove Farm and also for girls to ride down in their doll's pram (before mother took it away).

Possibly Moreton Mill Cottages 1949, pastel sketch by C S Fox

Next came the original mill house, which had been converted many years before to two cottages. These stood in a large area of ground surrounded by a moat, which was mostly silted up but still contained some water. To get to the cottages with dry feet, therefore, there was a raised footpath made from old millstones. James Vowles lived in one of these cottages – the other was unoccupied. The mill itself was long disused by then but its mill pool was a favourite spot for fishermen. From there, a footpath followed the Chew down to Stratford Bridge and provided a route on foot to Bishop Sutton. Lewis Cole, Arthur Derrick and James Vowles used the building for storage and other purposes. The owner of all these buildings was Sarah Keel.

Continuing south on Moreton Lane would bring you, on the left, to Yewtree Farm belonging to Clara Maggs, and shortly afterwards to James Stowell's Chestnut Farm. Both were small farms with few fields in addition to their orchards round the farm buildings.

Just beyond Chestnut Farm the lane forked, continuing as Moreton Lane on the left – the way to Stratford Lane. The fork to the right was Newclose Lane, which seemed to be a farm track or bridleway by 1938. Both of these met another lane (which still exists as a public footpath) crossing from the direction of Ubley, Nempnett and Moat Farm. The Moreton Lane traffic would turn left down this (unnamed) lane to reach Stratford Lane, the old Roman road that formed part of the parish boundary between Compton Martin and West Harptree.

Yew Tree Farm 1949, pastel sketch by C S Fox

Turning left at Stratford Lane would lead to Stratford Mill. Turning right would lead to the Blue Bowl Inn, almost immediately coming to the cottage belonging to John Loveridge and his family, with its pigsty and paddock. The Loveridges were Romanies and had visited the area for many years, camping along the wide grass verges along Stratford Lane before buying the cottage. The cottage was in Compton Martin parish and for practical purposes was regarded as part of Moreton.

CHAPTER SIX

Farming

The area covered in this study was an agricultural community. It was on the fringe
of the Somerset coal mining area and many men were employed at Bishop Sutton
Pit or at Bromley and Pensford. But farming was the dominant activity; not only
by being the major employer but also by generating work in service industries to
support it. Farming however, was not just the means of earning a living, it also
influenced every aspect of life within the valley. It is appropriate therefore that
we should first look at the type of farming which had developed in the area to
suit the local conditions.

We have collected the reminiscences of many people who grew up in Moreton
itself and among the maze of lanes and tracks that connected its outlying farms
and cottages to the wider reaches of the valley. Through their memories we can
look closely at the way things were when the idea of flooding the valley was first
put forward. It is impossible to categorise the inhabitants of the valley. Certainly
there are common factors and common problems, but the differences between
one family and another, one farm and another, are interesting and very
important.

By the time we reach the years that are within living memory in the 1930s we
find that the population of the hamlet of Moreton was around 70 (much as it is
believed to have been in Roman times). The whole of the valley was farmed,
though some of the low-lying land was still on the wet side.

The land was split between many farms. Some of these were owned by the
people who farmed them, but the majority were tenanted. Their sizes varied

between a few larger farms, some medium sized ones and others ranging down to some quite small farms. Denny Farm and Denny House Farm were examples of larger and medium sized farms, owned by families who were long established in the area. Moreton Farm was an example of a large tenanted farm, while Spring Farm, Lower Gurney Farm, Manor Farm and Herons Green Farm were perhaps of the next rank. Denny Hills Farm and Chew Park Farm were smaller tenanted farms. However, a farmer could increase the size of his holding by also renting another farm or even a number of individual fields.

We used to milk 45 to 50 cows. We farmed 230 acres. That was a big farm then.

There were several extensive and comfortable farms; some being owner occupied and others tenanted. Some tenancies, of good mixed farms, were highly prized, as the rents were considered low.

On the other hand in Moreton itself there were also small farms that must have provided at best a pitifully limited cash flow as family income, even though the people were by today's standards remarkably self-sufficient. These small farms commonly supported a herd of only seven or eight cows. Some people were determined to better themselves, though some degree of luck was required for success. A few holdings were in the occupation of World War 1 veterans who had been given the tenancy as a resettlement opportunity. One man recounted how his father started:

Father was a coal haulier at Sutton Pit but with his war pension purchased some land from George Russell. There was no background in farming but he built a house himself and built up a small farm. Pigs first of all and then finished up with everything dairy, pigs, and poultry. Everybody did a bit here in the valley, nobody specialised.

That farm developed successfully only to lose most of its land to the new lake. But not all starting out in farming were so lucky:

My Father was a water diviner and well sinker and he bought seven acres of land and built a house to have a little smallholding as a sideline sort of thing. But it was never a success. It was one of the worst things that he did. We had no luck at all; everything we touched went against success. He built state of the art piggeries and within two months had swine fever so no pigs could be kept on the land for quite a while. So he tried poultry. Normally young chickens got gapes but the older hens themselves got gapes there and we couldn't do anything. Then he tried market gardening and the bottom went out of the market and we were working for nothing.

The men and women we interviewed expressed a range of personalities and experiences. Individuals interact with their background and circumstances in many ways. In almost every case the underlying presence of love and family support softened the edges of hardship and an atmosphere of kindness and contentment generally prevailed. All farms were labour intensive and all but the smallest farm employed farm workers who occupied the farm cottages with their families. Most farm workers were happy with their work and very loyal to their employer but some workers moved jobs and therefore homes every few years. A record of the occupants of some farm cottages has been impossible to compile.

During the late 19th and early 20th century there had been many changes in farming. Hard physical labour and long hours were still there and applied to everyone, male and female, young and old, master and man. That was a fact of life. Nevertheless the introduction of new methods and machinery, beginning with horse drawn implements and later with tractors and tractor driven implements, reduced the need for manual labour and improved productivity. The transition from hand to machine milking had a similar effect, although many smaller herds were still being hand milked into the 1960s. One person could hand milk ten cows and in some cases they might milk twenty cows daily. But the younger generation had high expectations. John Curry told us of the time when he was left to milk their herd of 40 or 50 cows:

And do you know what, I milked the lot by hand. Father was gone to a show, or somewhere or other, and I done that twice. And I said to 'im, 'Now look, if you want those bloomin' cows like that you'll have to milk 'em yourself or get a milking machine'. And that's what made him get a milking machine.

Some farmers of course employed a cowman and although that was his principle responsibility he would obviously be called on to help at haymaking and harvest too. In those days when operations were so labour intensive farmers would help each other out on a reciprocal basis at peak times. At haymaking and at harvest and when there was threshing to be done the same people would be asked to come in and help and they could always be relied on. The whole family would give a helping hand as one woman remembered:

In those days it was just picks (forks) and loose hay. We used to go round with a hand rake and go all round the hedge. Then the baler came in and I used to sit on the baler because some of them would miss and I would have to tie them. I remember once when I got off my face was so dirty all they could see was my eyes. And the blouse I was wearing, I never got it out of the seams!

At harvest and at haymaking time local men were also available to work. Men from the local coal pits would sometimes help when they were off shift. In the summertime there was less demand for coal so they would be working short time. Miners were strong, capable, and willing and, not surprisingly, enjoyed work in the open fields for a change.

We had about 70 – 80 acres. My Dad employed two full time men. And there again you see, when it was haymaking you get the fellows that used to work in the mines. They would come in, say round teatime and help and then Mum, you know, used to take tea out in the hayfield. I don't think they got a lot of pay but they got their drop of cider and their tea.

Even the children would join in:

Curry's had two greys and we used to fight who would get up on their back and who would ride on top of the hay. We'd be there 'til eleven or twelve at night.

If things went well and the crop was safe the atmosphere was very congenial. Taking lunch and tea out to the haymakers was something the women did. The generous portions of homemade bread, cheese, pickles and cake were served with secret pride and much enjoyed by the hungry workers.

They used to have a huge basket with a lid, like they have for stage props. It would be filled with loaves of bread and cheese and pickle and great big flagons of cider. We all used to go, our Mother and all. It was lovely times. It's all gone now, all gone.

Cattle

Stock was the centre of the farmer's life, needing constant attention and care. Farming was a 24 hour business. Good stock sense was crucial. It meant having an eye that would spot an ailing beast at an early stage, forestalling trouble or the spread of infection. Most farmers had the knowledge to deal with calving and other problems. They would have a box full of traditional remedies for common maladies or injuries. Vets were only applied to in emergencies and often complained that they were called in too late to do any good. It was not unknown for an angry farmer who lost an animal after following the advice of a vet to tell him that he was never to set foot in his yard again!

One Vet lived in the valley and is well remembered:

Mr Prime at Chew Park House, he used to go around on horseback. He was a very smart man. He was a very good vet.

Originally in this part of the country the reigning breed of cattle were the

Shorthorns and a dairy strain was developed.

We had a pedigree Shorthorn herd. They were the general cattle in the area. There were very few of other breeds then but just occasionally you'd get the cross, you know. In fact, I think, when I was a young man, we only had the one Friesian until about 1959. Her name was Princess.

The Reads at Whitehall Farm liked cows with white backs. They were a Shorthorn cross with a white streak right from the back. Not many had cows like that.

We had names for all the cows; Lovely Broadhorn, Fillpail, Daisy, Primrose, and they knew their name more or less. There was this one cow, Daisy, and she would let nobody else milk her but Father. And if Father were to sit under another cow she would turn the other cow away.

William Hasell senior at Denny Farm with Shorthorn cows

They were red or roan with white and were horned and sometimes when with a calf a little uncertain in temper. One young girl, chaining up the cows in their stalls was pinned against the partition between the horns of an angry Shorthorn. It was always necessary to take care when sitting on a milking stool too as cows would sometimes kick. As for bulls, occasionally an attack might end in death and even the quietest could not be trusted entirely:

The bull was very important on the farm. We nearly always had a Shorthorn bull. On the whole they were good tempered but I had one that was nasty tempered. He and I fell out good and proper. He was at the back of his house and I was going in to do something with him and I had a five prong pick in my hand. So I put the pick over the door to open the door and he charged it. Being a five prong it was narrow and it went in his nose and he swished his head all round and blood all over the whitewash. He never forgot me. I had to watch him too. He was a rascal.

A farmer of a dairy Shorthorn herd remembered:

We never had too much in the beef line then. Generally we sold the bull calves to Mr Harris, Hinton Blewett. He was a calf dealer and his brother was another calf dealer. They used to come round and buy the calves direct from the farm and I've seen Father out in the yard arguing with Mr Stanley Harris over half a crown. Father wanted half a crown and he'd perhaps bid Father two and thruppence.

The Welsh used to buy the calves to fatten them out because they had the more open land. The calves would only be a week, ten days or a fortnight old perhaps. They stayed with their mothers till then.

During the forties some people kept Ayrshires and some people favoured the Channel Island breeds as they could get a premium for quality milk. Friesians were being introduced for pure dairy herds and after the war Canadian Holsteins – the ultimate gallonage providers. Pure dairy cattle were of little use as beef animals, and the crosses were not much sought after. Beef bulls could be brought on and some cows were kept as nurse cows with two or three calves at foot. Herefords were the most popular and Aberdeen Angus the best quality. After WW2 more and more continental breeds were imported. They attracted great attention at shows such as the Bath and West and began to appear on the more forward-looking farms. In the later years artificial insemination was used as this led to a better bred calf. A prize dairy bull could be chosen for the best cows in the hope of getting a choice heifer.

I can remember that my mother-in-law would never go round to the yard with the AI man as she found the whole thing very embarrassing. You had to take him a bucket of hot water and soap and a towel.

Dairy

In the 19th and early 20th century there had been a strong tradition of butter and cheese making, much of which was sold in Bristol. The need to market dairy produce led to a change in distribution. During the depression years the price was poor and economies of scale left small herds struggling. Help came with the establishment of the Milk Marketing Board, which provided a secure market.

We used to make cheese and we had it all stored for six months in the big cheese room and during that time we never had a penny for it. Then Father would take it to Highbridge market and it was sold for nothing at all really; you sold it for a few pence. When the Milk Marketing Board came in 1936 and took over we could sell the milk through them and be sure of our money.

Then there was pressure for the family farm to specialise in one enterprise. Those who were able to do so followed this trend whilst smaller and undercapitalised farms gave up the struggle. The Dairy at Chew Stoke became important to the local economy.

The milk was taken to the Dairy at Chew Stoke. The farmers used to take the churns to the depot themselves in the horse and cart or even on the back seat of their car! But then the Dury family started hauling milk around the area and taking it to the depot.

One farmer remembered a terrible accident just before the War:

They used to bring the milk out from the farm on to what we called a milk stand. John Patch, that was Edward Patch's brother, he put the milk on the milk stand. I don't know if it was snow or frost on the road but he was stood there and the milk lorry that came along to pick up the milk skidded and crushed him up against the milk stand.

In later years smaller churns holding only ten gallons replaced the twelve or seventeen-gallon ones!

The seventeen gallon churns didn't last too long, then it went back to the twelve gallons. The seventeen gallon churns they were heavy, mind. Ten or twelve is a different story.

Other farms had their own retail network and took the milk straight into town, at first in the churn and eventually in bottles. Either way milking took place twice a day on 365 days a year. A number of the people who grew up on farms have told us that they were expected to turn the cows out on their way to school and to bring them in for milking on the way back. Several had from one to four cows to milk too.

Hand milking was pleasant enough – it was a personal thing between you and the cow. They were all different. There were timid little heifers and hard old ladies with a swift and cunning kick. You sat so close in under them with a bucket between your knees and balanced on a little three-legged stool. If the cow was willing and a soft milker you soon got into a good rhythm and the milk in the pail had a good froth on it. Milking out in the ground was nice in the summer. Milking in the cow house was warm in winter but there wasn't much room between them.

During warm weather there was often a problem keeping the milk cool and fresh.

We used to stand our churns in the brook if it was hot and thundery.

The introduction of milking machines speeded up the job and a cooler improved the quality of the milk. But few of the valley farms were big enough to introduce such machinery as early as this farmer recalled:

I done the milking but by then we had a machine, a Vaccar. We had that one, I believe I'm right in saying, in 1934. There was a one and a half horsepower Lister petrol engine to power it. The cows went into stalls and then you carry it around with you. Generally, you had four buckets with four pulsators on and you would go round like that. It would take about an hour and a half. We had the cooler where the water goes through the cooler and the milk runs down outside and then it used to go into churns and then it went off. I had a cousin in Bristol that had a milk round and he had some of it and some of it used to go into a dairy.

There were schemes to improve the herd which forward-looking farmers could take part in. There was a price incentive to make sure you were free of cattle TB. It was voluntary but eventually it became law and it could come as a shock to discover that you had a few reactors. It wasn't obvious at all. You could also upgrade your herd and register as pedigree, but we never did it and I think it took several generations of cattle.

A Miss Taylor came to inspect dairy farms for their hygiene and procedures.

Miss Taylor worked for Somerset Farm Institute at Cannington. Oh, she was quite a character. Miss Taylor came even before Father had a milking machine, when we used to milk by hand. Father had a cheese maker and they'd been trained at Cannington and they would come and see the cheese maker and test the milk and see it was all done properly. She would take samples of the milk but not so often as what they do now. If you treated her right she was all right and then she would come round the farm once a year. But if you had any problems with your milk and the dairies complain then they'd be looking into it. If everything wasn't spot-on she would say straight away. She was a formidable lady. She was well known for that.

Another farmer recounted:

I remember Miss Taylor very well. She looked all round our buildings and said, 'What's all this decorations here?' That was cobwebs, that was! She was hot, she was very hot. She knew her job. Of course times have changed. I've seen the men smoking a cigarette and the ash going down in the milk!

Horses

There was one animal, the working horse, which was essential to the running of a farm but which has all but disappeared nowadays. Even a small dairy farm needed at least one horse for transport and for cultivation. Small farmers tended to keep a cob or 'half-way horse' as they were called. Larger farms and those with plough ground might have Shires. There was always some horse breeding and farmers would show at local agricultural shows.

We had a lot of horses on the farm. Father was one of the heads of the Keynsham Shirehorse Society. He bred a lot of colts, Shires, the heavy horses, and he had some good ones. He bred them to work but he sold them as well. He loved his horses. Pa and two or three farmers always used to go up and choose an entire (stallion) to come down from Forshaw's at Newark in Nottinghamshire. There was a big chap named Joe Gaskin, he was a great big fella who came down with the entire. The entire used to stand at Widcombe for a week, at the start of the season to get settled in, and then he'd go all round the district and then come back at the weekend to stand. The handlers used to have them all done up lovely with their manes and tails all curled up and tied.

Walter and Nelson Read with Shirehorse Mary at White Hall Farm c1938

Horses did not come ready-made and a lot of work went into schooling and training. However if a man was good with horses he could produce a good youngster for sale, another source of income. Men so often developed a great bond with the horses. They spent many hours in each other's company and became very attached. Where there was arable land, horses had more work to do over the seasons. Some farmers, such as George Curry, were dealers in horses:

> *Father used to deal in horses. We'd have 30 or 40 sometimes. A lot of horses came out of Bristol; George's Brewery and the coal rounds. They'd go wrong in their feet with the hard cobbles. We'd rest them for so long and then put them back to work or we'd sell them to other farmers.*

Sadly in many ways the introduction of tractors during and after WW2 caused the market for horses to disappear, for a horse had to be fed and cared for every day of the year, whereas an 'unemployed' tractor could be left in the barn.

> *But then the tractor came in. The first Fordson tractor we bought was in 1936. That was about the end of the heavy horses. Then we had a Case and the International. A lot of people forget that this country was built on the Shirehorse.*

Other livestock

Until after the War few farmers specialised in any one type of farming and therefore the mix of livestock was much wider than on a modern farm. Poultry and pigs were common throughout the valley while sheep were much less popular.

Pigs were kept on farms as well as by many cottagers who usually kept just one for their own use. In the case of farmers it was often an additional enterprise. Large Whites and Wessex were the most common and sometimes Tamworths, though after the War the Danish Landrace superseded other breeds. Many people kept a sow to farrow and others bought in a few weaners to fatten for pork or bacon. Many farmers killed one or more on the farm and took them to Bristol through a dealer or straight to a butcher. The procedure for killing a pig was a very familiar one. The throat was cut and the bristles burnt off over a fire of straw and the hide scraped.

> *We had the pigs and we used to have the whey from the cheese to feed the pigs. The person who used to come and kill the bacon pigs was a Rossiter Pool who lived at Hinton Blewett. Rossiter used to go round all the farms and he'd come back perhaps six or half-past six at night and he'd kill eight or ten pigs. He'd kill them with the pole-axe and cut them all up. When I come to think about it, it was a terrible job. Father would take them into Bristol the next day.*

Our Mum used to keep pigs. She used to take them up Norton Malreward to have them killed. They used to come back, the whole thing, in a muslin cloth. We had no fridge, so under the stairs our Dad hammered in some great big nails and that's where we hung them up. When our Mum wanted some bacon she would go out and slice some off, that's how we had to do it.

Poultry were very much the wife's concern. Cottagers usually kept just enough for themselves in a pen at the end of the garden. On farms the farmer normally paid the miller's bills. With 'free' grain his wife was able to produce an income of her own by hatching or buying in day old chicks and rearing them for the Christmas trade together perhaps with ducks, geese and turkeys.

Mum used to do the poultry. At Christmas time she used to do a lot of ducks and geese to sell. It was the woman's perks.

Older poultry breeds were Light Sussex and Rhode Islands and for egg production mainly Leghorns, but by the fifties there were new hybrid strains that were popular. Poultry of course involved busy days of killing and plucking and maybe dressing them for market. Everyone in the family might be asked to lend a hand. Flocks of free-range hens were the day to day source of 'pin money'. Eggs were either sold at the door or in a shop, or packed into egg trays and stacked in boxes and picked up by the Egg Marketing Board lorry. They had always to be carefully cleaned with a damp cloth and should on no account be washed! The shells are permeable and if they had been soaked in water the Egg Marketing Board would reject them. Keeping free-range poultry involved a lot of work. They were fed three or four times a day and morning and night it was a challenge to protect them from the fox and other predators.

The hens were all free-range. I can see'em now, about ten houses out in the home ground there and you used to push them forward a bit each day or every three or four days; a bit of fresh ground so it didn't kill the grass. They had to be closed in at night. We used to sell a few eggs at the door but generally we had a local chappie that used to come round and collect eggs from various farms and then take them to Bristol and sell them to the shops. It was difficult to keep the eggs clean and we broke a few!

There was Mr Lyons from Chew Park Farm, he used to come round picking up the eggs once a week and take them off.

Sheep were kept on the higher ground, the valley floor being rather wet for their welfare. Older ewes from the Mendips or elsewhere could produce an extra crop of lambs on the softer living of the valley. Breeds varied from Ryelands to Border Leicesters, Suffolks to Hampshire Downs, plus Scottish Halfbreds and a few Welsh or Kerry Hills. They were bought at Priddy Fair or Backwell to lamb the next spring or to fatten. Going to the sheep fair was a day out and a reunion of old friends and family. Not everyone had the skills to shear sheep and often someone was asked to come and assist. Lambing was an anxious time too. You needed skill and patience to deliver twins or triplets badly presented and tangled one with another. The ewe could so easily go into shock and you could lose her as well as the lambs. Furthermore ewes so often chose to lamb on the coldest and stormiest night of the year.

> *There weren't many sheep in the area then. We had only 40 or 50. We used to have the sheep up on the hill and I used to spend hours on that hill walking with my collie dog. We had no Landrover then! Sometimes I rode horseback round there but I got tired of doing that – having to open the gates and getting over the rails. I always had a good dog.*
>
> *They were generally a cross from the Welsh mountains. But they were terrible roamers, mind. I like the Suffolk 'cause they're quiet and they don't get out and roam around but the cross were perhaps more hardy and more milky. We used to fatten the lambs and they go to market. The fleece was worth something then. Today it don't even pay for the shearing. I can remember seeing the hazels cut and made into hurdles for them.*
>
> *We had to inform the police when we were going to dip the sheep and he would come and see it done.*

Vermin

The countryside however also supported other animals, which were not always welcomed by the farmers. The farm cats and dogs controlled rats and mice and foxes were hunted. But there were other pests:

> *Our biggest problem was rabbits and the rabbits were absolutely terrible. You can't believe what rabbits we had. You couldn't move for rabbits. We had no grass. I used to do a lot of rabbiting myself. I kept a polecat and I always had three ferrets at home and we could go out an afternoon and catch 70 rabbits. We would put a loose ferret down a hole, put nets all round and the ferret would drive the rabbit. You had to be down the net and catch the rabbit coming out but you had to be very quick, mind, 'cause there was always another one behind generally. I enjoyed that.*
>
> *Mother used to always fry rabbits. We had bacon and cream, that was beautiful that was – always young rabbits.*
>
> *Father was a good shot and he was walking round the hill with me one night and he killed, I think it was, seven rabbits with one shot. When I was young we had so many as that. We picked up the two or three young ones and threw the old ones in the hedge.*

In 1939 Dr Brew, who had the shoot at Widcombe, always engaged a resident keeper all the time then. This particular keeper they had, his name was Wilfred Haynes generally lived in the cottage down Monksilver. He caught 4000 rabbits on our farm alone from the September 'til the April. Wilf Haynes knew his job so well. His wife was a little tiny person but she could shoot as well as he could. What he would do, he would do a hedge. He would do it methodically. He'd stand one side and his wife the other and he'd turn the rabbits out with his dog. Then after that he'd net them, ferret them. And what he didn't get with the ferret he'd trap. He really cleaned that hedge right out like that.

They were beginning to come back again in the late forties early fifties. Myxomatosis was introduced from Australia. That was wicked. I don't believe in suffering. They had it so bad because they couldn't see. The crows picked their eyes out. It was horrendous really. The smell on our hill was dreadful.

Animal feed

Most of the valley land was either rich pasture grazed by the cattle in summer or meadow that provided hay. In the winter, this was the staple diet of cattle as well as horses. On livestock farms, such as those in the Chew Valley, the health and very survival of the animals depended on a supply of good hay. The nutritional quality, however, varied from season to season and from sample to sample. This

Haymaking at Widcombe 1923 Colston Gay, Alfred Gay, ? on the wagon

is why so much care was taken to 'make it right' and other foods were made to balance and enrich it.

The land was rich and if set aside for hay early in the season produced a heavy crop. It was essential to choose the right day to cut it when the glass was set fair. There were many stages to be processed before the hay was secure. The aim was to get it dried and hauled before the weather broke and long days were necessary to do that. In the early days, working with horse gear and hand tools, progress was slow and gradually farmers had to buy new equipment to speed up this crucial work. Typically there was a tractor-drawn mowing machine, a swathe turner, a sweep to bring the hay to the collection point and an elevator to load it on a trailer or finally on to the mow. These were investments and a farmer bought as much as he could prudently afford. The dread of a disastrous haymaking season loomed large and there was great relief when the next winter's feed with all its nutrients was safely in hand.

The mixing of feed for animals was of importance too. There were changes here over time and between the war years there were imports of cattle cake and molasses to help balance the diet. This made it possible to keep more cows to the acre and so increase the size of the herd.

We used to grow vetches years ago to feed the cattle. And we used to grow mangels (a large kind of beet) and swedes. We had a grinder to chop them up. You could put them in as fast as you like, it would grind them up. I used to enjoy that job. And then we had the chaff-cutter. That was a dusty old job because it was always the poorest hay or straw you would put through the chaff cutter and mix the mangels with it and beet pulp which we bought and sometimes molasses. Mix it up and feed the cows like that and they used to clean it up fairly well then. That's all completely out today.

Silage was new technology before the War and was taken up more and more by those who could afford to invest in the big trailers and storage clamps. It was a less risky crop than hay as it could be saved even in a wet season. It could be smelly but it had good feed value. The grass was cut earlier than hay and hauled whilst it was still green. I don't think many of the valley farms were geared up for it. We never had it because of the uncertainty of the future; we couldn't risk the investment.

Foot and Mouth disease

A major problem when it occurred was an outbreak of Foot and Mouth disease. It caused some disruption to the entire community and anxiety on every farm. A good herd of cattle that had been built up over the years, perhaps over several generations was a precious asset. Furthermore, in those days, when herds were smaller and every cow had a name known to all the family, their loss was almost personal. Destruction was heartbreaking and having been in contact, all other stock on the farm was under sentence, including the farm dog which had been a good friend. There were some hard cases as a woman vividly recounted:

Dad's animals didn't have it but because Dad had let the neighbouring farmer's cow, that was having difficulty calving, come into our shed he had to have all his animals destroyed as well. I remember a big Irish man came to do the destroying. There was a lot of people about. It was dreadful because all the heads and bits of bodies were thrown on the lawn outside the house and the hides were hanging on the railings. The smell was awful, it really was. It was ghastly. And of course we had to dip our feet in the trough as we came in the end gate. And our little pet lamb sat under the kitchen table, couldn't be moved, but we knew what was coming.

One could have bought one in and they could have come from an infected herd. You used to go into Bristol Market and buy these Irish cattle and they were prone to get it. Father's brother had it on his farm when the war started. We were very, very lucky not to have had it. All the cattle were taken and slaughtered and those that were all right went for human consumption because of the War. Only about eight or ten were burnt on the farm.

The local police were involved too as a retired policeman remembered:

The disease created a lot of problems because a vast area, miles around the affected farm would be made a standstill. The animals on that particular farm with the outbreak would be slaughtered and so there was a job to supervise the burning of these animals. Any movement in that restricted area had to be done under licence and the licence was issued by the police officers.

Arable land

The soil of the pasture and meadow land on the valley floor was often heavy and wet. During the 19th century a few farms grew teasels which thrived in these conditions. They were grown as a cash crop which was transported north to the mill towns. There they were set into wooden frames for combing the woven cloth. Daisy Maggs recounted to us what her husband told her:

Grandfather grew acres of teasels on the Chew Stoke side of Moreton, which he hauled to Gloucester by wagon and horses. Mr Payne who used to live in Chew Stoke, he would say if he heard a wagon going off early in the morning, 'That must be Sid Maggs going off to Gloucester'.

By the 1930s although some crops were grown to supply cattle feed, mainly kale and roots, there were few farms that had either suitable land or indeed the equipment (or even the skills) necessary to grow cereals. A farmer on the edge of the valley recalled:

I wouldn't say Father was quite typical of the Chew Valley, not then, because he always had some arable, whereas a lot of them couldn't. They had a hay crop, great big ricks of hay, and they'd grow some mangels, swedes and kale, all for the animals and potatoes for their own use.

We'd grow mangels or swedes or vetches for sheep or for the cattle. We had three pieces of arable. That would have been at the most 30 acres of arable and we grew nearly all barley for the animals and some wheat which we always sold. We had our own (small) *mill or, if we couldn't cope, we'd take the barley to the local mills and get it ground; barley meal for pigs or rolled barley for to feed the fat cattle. And we would take some wheat as well, seconds wheat or oats.*

But Father used to buy a lot of barley and maize, whole maize and I know a lot of this came from Persia. It came so cheap. I think it was imported for £4 a ton! I can remember buying linseed cake at £14 a ton which was terribly cheap really.

Father farmed his three with rotation. One field every year was fallow to keep it clean and there was never no thistle or docks. We would plough it three or four times, let the air into it and kill any weeds, not to need any spraying. My father always said, 'To summer fallow a piece of land and plough it three or four times was equal to giving it a good coat of manure'. We mostly used farmyard manure but we did use a bit of fertiliser. You could get basic slag (a by-product from iron smelting, high in phosphates) *and things like that.*

Machinery

Up until the 1930s farming tools were very basic. Most farms would have a plough and horse hoe for arable:

Mangel and swede hoeing; you would have the horse hoe and someone would lead the horse and he would hoe two rows at once. That was quite a popular thing.

There was a great art in ploughing. My Father was a good ploughman with horses. He knew how to set the plough and he was an expert and he showed me how to do it.

If a farm had arable ground it needed arable tackle or they had to get a contractor to do the work for them. They might or might not have a reaper binder. Then they would need a seed drill and fertiliser spreader. It was a bit of an investment. It was important to start with a good tilth and good germination and growth. Then when the corn was in ear and had ripened it had to be cut and dried and hauled, as and when the weather permitted, and often there wasn't a minute to spare for every drop of rain lowered the quality of the crop.

We used to go down there (Moreton) either mowing or harvesting. Cole's, Lewis Cole, we used to go down there. Most of them got their own tractors for light work but for the corn cutting you'd have the binder. It wasn't worth while the farmer spending several hundred pounds for a binder, so we'd go in and have to set it all up. Let the big wheel down and then put the sheets down and put the wind mill on, so as 'e cuts it, so 'e knocks it back on the sheet. Then that goes up like that, between two sheets and then gets tied in a bundle and thrown out the back in a stook. And then people come behind and stook them up 'till it had dried, then that was all picked up on a trailer and you'd make a round mow. Usually they put down bits of stick, to make like a foundation to keep it off the ground and then they built the mows up on them and then thatched them.

I only ploughed with horses at home but as soon as Father bought the tractor in 1935 then I went on the tractor because you could do so much more.

Lewis Cole threshing at Grove Farm

When we bought the plough, it was a Ramson, and their theme was that a man called Fosset, a Yorkshireman, he was champion ploughman of England three years in succession, he came and gave me a few tips; how to set it and what to do. I had a two-furrow plough to start with, then it was three and now they're huge.

Other than on the largest of farms, the threshing of corn had always been contracted out to one-man businesses. He would employ one man to help him but each farm had to provide another seven or eight men to help. Threshing machines had been powered by steam traction engines which required huge quantities of coal from the local pits and water from farm ponds and streams. They were extremely noisy and sooty but immensely impressive and created excitement wherever they went. But the tractor could power a threshing machine and do countless other jobs. The tractor therefore ended the age of steam and horsepower on the farm and started the gradual reduction of manpower.

During the War years there was a big increase in corn growing at the insistence of the Government.

Everybody was ploughing; everybody had corn because of the War. I came and ploughed 60 to 70 acres for Uncle and I did our own at Widcombe as well. I was ploughing (for other farms) night and day for a long time. We had great difficulty getting our threshing done. And when we couldn't get a threshing machine Father decided we would try and get one of our own.

In 1941 they bought a machine, a Clayton, south of Dorchester and they brought it back towed behind their tractor, a Case D. The Case wasn't powerful enough to power the thresher and so they got a Lease-Lend tractor, an International Harvester. (Lease-Lend was an arrangement by which means America provided essential machinery and goods during WW2.)

When I started threshing, I didn't get any peace at all. People were asking for me to come and thresh some corn for them all the time. We had an area allocated by the Agricultural Committee and we were supposed to stick strictly to that. I had the parishes of East and West Harptree, Compton Martin, Litton, Hinton Blewett, Clutton and Temple Cloud. Threshing could be done throughout the year. I'd start as soon as we started to cut the corn, say the last week in July, August time, and I'd thresh then non-stop right up 'till perhaps the first week in the following June, right through the year. Some people would keep their wheat until June because the price would be a bit better, you see.

All the corn grown down in the valley that they had, they brought it up on the hard ground near to the road in ricks and I threshed up there. (The land by the river was liable to flooding and being wet in winter, it was not suitable for growing corn. Land that was slightly higher could grow it but instead of building the rick where it was cut it was brought back to the yard where it was drier.) *During the War, I threshed continuously until 1948. I didn't do any of any consequence after that, only those who wanted it for thatching or the straw. The combines started to come in and that finished it.*

Tractors were starting to come into their own and trailers were converted from horse tackle (various binders, collectors, elevators, mowers, etc.). The farmer and his workers had to move from the care and handling of horses to acquiring the mechanical knowledge necessary to maintaining a tractor:

The fuel they used was TVO which was like paraffin. But you'd start them on petrol 'cause TVO wasn't strong enough to ignite. The Fordson had a big tank on the top of the tractor for TVO and a small one at the back that would hold about a gallon of petrol and a two-way tap underneath. Well then, when you start up in the morning you make sure your tap's turned on, bottom of the carburettor undo the screw there, drain off any TVO that's in there, turn the petrol on until it comes through, switch off and then start up. And a lot of time you start up and forget to turn over to TVO and suddenly 'e stops. Oh blimey! Of course 'e got nice and hot, so you get on straight away and turn the handle and 'e fired on TVO so you had to keep 'im running all day. At night the manifold would all be a cherry-red glow, red-hot. They'd make you cuss sometime. Each tractor had its knack of starting, you know. None of this turning a key in the ignition. And what we used to do, just above the intake of the carburettor there was a screw which you'd be able to unscrew and you would have an oil can with petrol in, squirt that in there and that would be sucked direct into the engine. So you didn't have to do too much turning (of the starting handle) before 'e fired up. And of course, it was a big magneto, no batteries or anything, which clicked around like that. Each click a darn great spark came off the end of the leads of the plugs.

A former land girl (women conscripted to do farm work during WW2) clearly remembered working with tractors:

We had Ford tractors but not always the same one. Most of the tractors had solid wheels with spade lugs, which dug into the ground, but some of them, for lighter work, had pneumatic tyres. The seat was sprung so it wasn't too uncomfortable. It wasn't too bad to drive but the hardest part was the foot brake 'cause that was up pretty high. You had to sort of put your whole weight on it to get it down to the floor if you wanted the tractor to stop.

I travelled ten miles sometimes to get to jobs going at about five miles an hour. It had four gears, three and one in reverse. Before it could go on the roads they had to have four blocks put on each wheel. You had to clean all the mud off before you fitted the blocks. They fitted between the spade lugs and a bolt at each end went through one of these holes in the wheel and you had to put a nut on the inside. The wood was curved but it had like a metal rim to it because the wood wouldn't last long on the roads. Sometimes you would be going along with these blocks on and one of the bolts would snap.

We did ploughing on our own. You had to pace it out and put a stick up one end of the field, which you drove straight for. If you kept that stick in line with the cap of the radiator then your line would be dead straight. You would measure out so many paces and then you would start another one.

Orchards

There is one further facet of farming in the valley which was important and which has all but disappeared today, the orchard. Looking down on a village it would be almost hidden by fruit trees, a haze of pale pink in blossom time. There were all kinds of fruit; apples, pears, plums, greengages and damson. The soft fruit was bottled and the apples and pears, if carefully stored, provided fruit for cooking and eating in most months of the year. But the main crop was for cider which was consumed in varying quantities by the family and the staff.

Quite a few of the farms did make their own cider. They made it for themselves and the staff. Back before the war Showerings at Shepton bought in apples. (A farm that didn't make its own cider could still receive an income from its orchards.) We had our orchards and my Father always made his own cider until the apple trees had gone past it. I would have thought we stopped it in the early thirties. The orchards had to be maintained and kept up together and I suppose the cost of it didn't warrant it and the staff weren't drinking the cider that they used to.

I can remember my Father had a couple of staff and they'd get as drunk as fiddlers. They'd have a job to walk home. It was dangerous. They all liked their cider. Father would have a glassful every night for supper regular, but in later years he gave it up. Cider was a big thing. If a man (farm labourer) had his wage of £1 12s 6d he also expected cider. They would drink all they wanted during the day and they would always take a quart or so home with them for supper. They didn't go to the pub much they couldn't really afford to. We had a person working for us for many, many years. He'd drink a pint of cider just like that, and he'd be milking and he'd go in the cider house, get a pint of cider, down with it and go on milking again. Cider killed a few. It's very potent.

Of course there were some lovely orchards at Denny. My Father always made cider in a real old-fashioned cider press in the cider house across the yard. In the cider house you had the press there and there was a big stone trough with the lip and then the barrel was down underneath to collect it. And then down under the house there was the cellars where they used to take the cider in wooden barrels. The genuine cider apples made the best cider.

The variety of apples was enormous and many are now lost to us. Everyone knew which ones were good for eating or cooking or for cider:

Most orchards had an apple called Underleaves and we had a lot in our orchard. They were good cookers and they were good cider apples as well. We grew Morgan Sweets; they were lovely, you never hear of them now. We had Tom Putts, they were red ones. There was Beauty of Bath and Kingston Blacks. That was the best cider apple. You only make good cider with good apples, mind.

Markets

Market day was often appreciated as a diversion from the daily routine of the farm. There were often calves to sell, or a dry cow or weaned-off pigs or whatever. Or a farmer may have been looking around for an addition to his own herd. Going to market had a serious purpose as far as profit was concerned but there was more to it than that. There was companionship; a man was among his peers and it could be a social support. Farming could be an isolated business and the weekly market was something to look forward to:

Tuesdays was Winford Market and my Father would have some calves or some lambs to go to market and they always went in the horse and cart and I would drive the horse and cart to market when I was sixteen or seventeen. If they were good lambs you could put in six or eight, lift them in, and then we would have a net over them, and we would have as many as five or six calves. It was a crank cart; the axle went down so it was lower. I would take them regular to Winford, book them in, put them in the pens and then I would take the cart back up to Church Farm, to Mr Russell's farm, and take the horse out of the cart and in the stable and rest. This would be say eleven o'clock and he would stay there 'til market was over, half past three or four o'clock, and I would come back and get the horse and cart and come back home through the lanes.

We sent the animals to Winford. Ted and John used to drive them, on foot. They wouldn't do that now. But then, there wasn't anything on the road.

In the market, waiting for a likely beast to enter the ring or relaxing after business was satisfactorily completed, you would chat to a friend or distant cousin, commiserate when prices were poor or the weather 'catchy', perhaps pass on a bit of local gossip. Men found that their problems were not peculiar to themselves after all. There was laughter and congenial company to send a man home in a jovial frame of mind. He wasn't going to get breathalysed and the horse knew the way!

In the early days there were mostly fairs. I mean there was Ubley Fair, Blagdon Fair, Compton Martin Fair. Every little village had a fair, including Priddy of course. Winford started in about 1900 behind the Waterloo in an orchard, it was just a calf auction then, and in 1910 they moved to the other side of the road opposite the Waterloo, where the new development is.

In those days there were lots and lots of markets. There were markets at Winford, Farrington, Weston, Yate, Thornbury, Yatton and Keynsham. All had markets and now all those have gone. In those days stock had to be driven there. They started where there was a local trade, then they developed where there was a railway, Keynsham market did and Highbridge, Shepton Mallet, and Frome market. Then of course road transport came in and that's when Winford started growing very fast. Everybody had a lorry then so that's how it developed from there. Then of course it outgrew itself and moved to the present site in 1974. And now of course it's defunct. Shame, isn't it.

Changes are of course inevitable. Nothing remains the same forever. Some of the changes that we have seen fill many with regret and sadness at the thought of what has been lost. Yet they have mixed feelings about the loss of the small farms in the valley. Few of them would be viable in the present day. This is not due to lack of enterprise or effort but to changing patterns of food production and marketing. The reduction in the number of farm businesses on the valley floor would have taken place in any event. At least they have not survived in a state of neglect and dereliction. The lake has now matured into a very beautiful and productive environment in its own right. It is just that, looking back, what has taken place in the farming world has thrown into high relief the contrast between the way farming was then and the way it is now. It was a very different way of life and after all not everything has changed for the worse.

CHAPTER SEVEN

The Home

Within the valley there was a wide range of habitations. Well-built farmhouses were appreciated and farm labourers would think themselves lucky to have 'a good cottage', as some of them were very damp and 'tumbledown'. The living accommodation was certainly a consideration when moving to another farm, although it was often said that 'the house didn't matter, it was the land that you got your living from'! Two women remembered their childhood homes and accepted them as just the way things were:

There was no windows in the house, they was all boarded up. If you had nine children you couldn't do much. We had pump water, no sink, but a bowl to wash up in. We had no electric but oil lamps and candles. You couldn't see a lot could you? We was off to bed by eight o'clock. We had a wooden toilet seat with a bucket under it that had to be tipped out and buried.

We had water. We had a toilet up the garden with a wooden seat. Every night, after school we all had our jobs to do, I had to scrub the toilet seat! We had a big garden all at the front (of the cottage). We had some fruit trees as well. Grandad had his half and we had ours. He used to come over and pinch ours because his didn't grow so well. His name was George Tucker.
We only had this boiler in the corner of the kitchen that our Mum used to do her washing in. She used to light the fire under and she used to cook the Christmas puddings in it. On the top she would cook the potatoes on a Primus. We had an open fire she would cook the cabbage on, the saucepans

Moreton Cottages, Granny and Grandad Tucker with Pam, Mike and Terry c1952

got black. It had an oven on the side and a little oven at the top. We used to keep the stick (lighting wood) *in that to keep it dry and a piece of wire round the mantelpiece to hang your socks on to dry. I wish I had some photos. We had some great times. Those times are gone now.*

Other houses had rooms that could not be used because the floors were unsafe. On the other hand there was the lovely Woodford House, 'a gentleman's place'.

Every home was different but the following description of the house at Grove Farm, Moreton illustrates the type of living conditions common to most properties up until the first half of the 20th century:

If you came in through the front door to the hallway and turned left you would go into the big best room; Sundays only, with a fire and a green tiled fire grate, flagstone floors, very nice furniture, some beautiful vases and things. The stairs led to the front bedroom. Then you turn right into the big kitchen. And it was, with a whacking great big table, the big inglenooks with ovens either side and all the stick and the chumps (split logs for burning), *the fire grate with a little tiny fender in front and a rag rug. I can never remember a guard going over it. Mother cooked on it. She had nowhere else. She had the hobs either side and she would pull them over with the saucepans on. She did some lovely meals as well. And then there was a big settle which took the draught. And if you went behind the settle you could go up the back stairs, then into the back bedroom and into another room that went over the dairy but you didn't go in there because the floorboards were unsafe.*

In the kitchen we had the sink and then there was a whacking great big chest of drawers. Huge, I couldn't even get it open; two drawers at the top and then long ones, and above that there was a big hunting scene, 44 horses and dogs that I could never count. And then you would go, also behind the settle, and you would drop down a step and there was the big back door but then that put you out into a back kitchen sort of thing. It was where the coal was kept under the stairs and another door opposite opened up and that was the dairy. But it wasn't a dairy where the milk was. It was where you sorted the pigs and chitterlings and hang things up, a cold store like a pantry where things were kept under wire mesh.

But just before you went into that doorway there was a stone sink and you would have your bowl of water and put it there and wash there. Mum would have the kettle on the stove and the enamel bowl would be in the sink and she would bring the kettle over. It would always be just the right temperature.

Through the big back door then and then you were into a concreted area almost. There was the pump and there was a copper boiler under a lean to. The copper was used for the washing. Monday was wash day but when my grandfather became ill, a stroke, every day was wash day. Here too was where Mr Martin, Chew Stoke, delivered our coal. And then there was a wide pathway going on up into the yard. And that was where the pig was killed and all the blood ran down into the drain. And then you walked out through there (approximately 50 metres), Grandad would put down planks of wood, and that was where the toilets were. But you didn't use them in the night. We had our potties under the bed!

We would have a tin bath in front of the fire once a week. We would all share it but I got it first, then Mum did. We put the towels on the chairs to warm in front of the fire. Mum would have the kettles on the stove steaming away.

We had oil lamps and candles. The kitchen was a dark room, only lit up at night by the one oil lamp which sat on the table.

It was flagstones out in the kitchen, in the best room and the hall and they had to be scrubbed but it was lino through all the bedrooms.

There was only three bedrooms which led into each other but there was a staircase either side. My parents had the main bedroom, I shared the middle one and the third one was occupied by the live in lodger. I had a feather bed and feather pillows and a patchwork quilt.

Heating and lighting

Some conditions were common to everyone, right across the social spectrum.

Open fires of coal or wood heated even the more prosperous farms. A kitchen range was usual, and later cooking stoves such as Rayburns and Agas, either solid fuel or oil-fired, were prized.

Although we had our range going, it wasn't the warmest of houses. But Mother always had a good fire going.

You just had one fire. The house was absolutely freezing and you'd go to bed in the bitter cold and you couldn't get to sleep it was so cold, no heat in the bedrooms. I remember ice on the inside of the windows. And you had to light the fire in the morning before you could get a cup of tea. You had to do it.

Candles and oil lamps supplied the light at night. The best ones were Tilley lamps, which had a mantle and gave a good warm light. Out of doors there were pressure lamps which could be carried across the yard and into the cow house. By the late 1930s the larger farms had generators to power milking machines. The generator was then used in the evenings to provide electric lighting within the house. This was a wonderful development.

Water and drainage

None of the properties demolished to make way for the lake had a mains water supply. Water had to be drawn from a well or spring and carried into the house or dairy in enamel buckets. And then of course there was the rainwater butt that supplied soft water for washing clothes and for baths and hair. If you were lucky you might have your own well, with or without a pump, in the kitchen or cellar – or outside the house altogether. Some houses had a well that was shared between several and these included the first council houses built in Chew Stoke as one resident remembered:

We moved to a Council house in 1930 but we didn't have running water. We had a communal well and we used to have to go along with buckets and things. And these buckets were heavy but you accepted it. It was a way of life.

Every one of the people we interviewed had similar vivid memories of the effort involved in obtaining water. Nowadays we take for granted that it will pour continuously from our taps but things were very different then.

In the summer our spring was running so slow that I used to take the old terry napkins down to the brook and stand up to my shins and let the water run through them to rinse the soap out.

We had to go to the farm to carry water for drinking and that. We did have a big tank to help out for washing. If we hadn't had any rain and you wanted to go washing you just had to go to the farm and carry it down to the boiler.

Some men did plumb in a cold tap to a storage tank but there was still a great deal of effort required to manually pump the water up to the tank and often this was the housewife's job!

Well, Dad fixed up a pump to pump the water up and we had tanks up over so that we could have taps. But then that was cold taps, not hot taps. All the water was heated in the copper. Mum lit the copper every day. You had to light the copper because you wanted hot water for washing the milk things. And of course you had to pump the water up first of all.

Hot water, including that required for scouring milk churns and buckets could only be supplied by heating it over a fire either in kettles or in a copper boiler, so the fire had to be kept going winter and summer. An expected chore for many children was to scavenge for stick. Open fires made a lot of work.

Fires were hard work; you take in all the wood and the stick and then you got to take all the ashes out. A room had to be thoroughly cleaned every day then. You couldn't just go round with a duster and get away with it. And then of course they (the chimneys) had to be swept in the springtime.

There was an old lady here, she used to set fire to the chimney instead of sweeping it. Over the years she had nearly burnt through the ceiling joists!

Neither was main drainage in place. A couple of the houses in the valley had inside toilets, the contents of which went to a cesspit, but most homes had primitive toilet facilities. Usually these were at the bottom of the garden and in most families the men avoided using them. They had access to the fields and hedgerows and did not wish to clean out the pits more often than necessary.

The toilet, that was up the garden with a big seat and a little seat. It all dropped down... and it had to be cleaned out. And grandfather would never use it. He always went back behind the barn somewhere and my Mother always told me never to go back behind the barn after lunch! That's the way it was.

Washing and cleaning

In spite of these inconveniences respectable people kept themselves clean.

We had baths in front of the fire in a tin bath, the usual thing in those days. Friday night was bath night and that meant our hair as well. The little one was always first and I was always last. Mum used to always wash our hair with rainwater.

And although clothing was made of natural fabrics and was rarely colourfast when washed, that too was taken care of. One farmer's wife who had a large family between 1908 and 1920 was proud to boast to her daughter-in-law that none of her children 'ever wore a stitch of anything but white before they were seven years old'. You see, white could be boiled. There were of course no tumble dryers and a wet wash day meant wet clothing and linen draped everywhere.

Wash day was a real job. I remember Sundays, after we had been to church we used to have to carry the water into the house, fill the boiler up and then all the baths that we had, so that Mother would have plenty of water to do the washing on Monday.

She had a hard life really. On a Monday she would be up at about six o'clock to get the copper going and then she would wash and starch it. She was quite short and she used to have to stand up to rub the clothes with the scrubbing board. And she had this great big line right across the orchard to dry the washing. All day Monday practically was washing. Then Tuesday was the ironing day. So it really was hard work.

There were of course no electric irons. The flat-irons were heated on the fire or range, removed with a cloth holder, wiped clean, and used as swiftly as possible before they lost all their heat. The ironing was done on a folded blanket on the kitchen table and you tested the heat of the iron by holding it near your cheek or by spitting on it. Minor burns were frequent and so was scorched linen.

Neither were there any other electrical items such as refrigerators, vacuum cleaners or dishwashers. Everything had to be done by hand. Butter was handmade in an old wooden churn and shaped by wooden pats. The kitchen range was kept in a high state of polish by the blacking brush. The wooden table where all meals were taken had to be scrubbed daily. It was the only working surface for the preparation of meals, baking, preserving fruit and vegetables as well as for ironing, sewing and writing. The rugs and bits of carpet were shaken by hand or beaten over the clothesline, because they got so dusty. Blue-stone flags looked lovely, but they were laid on beaten earth and had to be scrubbed carefully without getting them too wet.

Despite the women's best efforts some of the old buildings were difficult to keep free of household pests. One man remembered the problems a neighbour had with cockroaches:

The old lady up there, she used to put down Keatings powder every night and sweep them up in the morning – shovelfuls – and put them on the fire.

Then of course all farms had problems with mice and rats:

Rats came from the river, and of course there was meal about. It was handy to have cats and dogs that would catch a rat.

Other females in the family were usually expected to help as a matter of course.

Often the eldest daughter stayed off school on a Monday. When old enough to leave school she remained at home to help her mother. Even quite modest households employed help in the home. Several women talked about this:

Latterly she had help. Fanny used to come and help Mum with the washing and the bedrooms and that sort of thing and sometimes she would milk. She was a general dogs-body really.

My Mother always had someone to help in the house, whatever needed to be done. When we were very small we had a girl live in and after that we had a woman from the village.

Farmers' wives were proud of their standards and Mrs Holbrook at Herons Green was best known for her spectacular display of china and the perfection of her housekeeping. This was mentioned by every one that we spoke to who had ever visited their farm. Arthur Young, a great source of information concerning the way things were, recalled:

I used to go there hoeing mangolds (another name for mangels) *and picking up apples. We'd be working and then about lunch time he'd come out and he'd say 'Come on up then and have your vitals' and old Mrs Holbrook 'ud put up a dinner, well, enough to feed a navvy really. She were a good one for food down her place. As to her china, I'd never seen anything like it. She had a dresser as big as eight foot wide and nearly as high. And I don't know how many services there were. I never saw anything to match it. And the house, that were spotless! It had to be seen to be believed. You'd never believe, and for a farmhouse too!*

Cooking and food

A woman remembered the difficulties her mother had to overcome to cook family meals:

All the cooking was done on Primus stoves or the open fire because there was no cooker as such. Although she did have an old oil-fired range but it was very difficult to control. But she used to turn out some lovely meals. We did have a coal-fired range but we didn't use that one because it smoked so. And so Mum did the vegetables on Primuses and the potatoes used to go on the sitting room fire and sometimes when you moved them too quickly it would all end up in the fire and put the fire out.

Everyone, without exception, who we have talked to, has recalled the quality and abundance of their food in those days. Most people say they had butcher's meat once or twice a week. Others, where they were in farming, killed their own. There were pigs on a regular basis, as well as lambs and calves on some occasions.

There were old hens, and sometimes chicken, and there were rabbits and game and the occasional fish. Hedgerow fruits, nuts and mushrooms were harvested and made good use of:

We kept rabbits and things. Poultry – if you were short of cash, you could always get a hen and knock her on the head. People think that's dreadful these days! Pigs too, all of them kept a pig or two. If you had a bit of ground you just might keep a cow for a drop of milk and perhaps it would have a calf and you'd sell that or bring it on. We were never short of vegetables and with chickens and that, if you had an egg you could always make a meal. We had fruits off the trees. We ate rabbits, oh we did! I can't face 'em now we did have so many!

Killing the pig

Everyone kept pigs, what today would be a large white. There wasn't really a breed. We went in those days for a big fat pig that weighed about fourteen stone. You fattened up the piglet, then killed it in November or December and that would last you through hopefully. And then you had another pig going. The kitchen was here and the pig was next door. In the kitchen we had a side of bacon hung up. A man came in to do the killing and dressing of it. You put it in a bath and keep it covered in salt to cure it.

We had trout from the river and a good garden. We didn't have much of anything but we all used to set to the table and you all had to sit there till it was finished. Nowadays some people don't even have a table. If we had a bottle of Heinz tomato sauce that was a treat and we hadn't to take too much. And a tin of fruit was a treat on a Sunday – or a tin of salmon. That was a great treat.

Food was largely seasonal and much depended on preservation and storage. Potatoes, roots and apples could be kept for months, eggs could be stored in water-glass, and fruit such as plums were bottled. There were shelves full of jams and pickles. Most women would make dozens of puddings at Christmas, boiling them in the wash copper, all wrapped in scalded cloths. They were held in reserve for the days when there was only cold meat for dinner. Cakes and puddings were made on most days and much relished.

When there was an animal killed nothing was wasted as people made sausages, brawn, chitterlings, bacon and preserved the hams. Some made their own bread. Butter might well be made on a regular basis and even cheese, and surpluses could be sold to form part of the family income. Farmers' wives were very busy people indeed! Even in wartime country people lacked for very little as they took good care of their own needs. Cooking was a constant activity and many of the women had levels of skill that were much appreciated and were passed down from mother to daughter. Looking back at it all, they are amazed at how hard their mothers worked.

We had a Jupiter stove for cooking and an open fire. He made sure we had plenty of good food. That was one thing he did do. We did have a rabbit or a piece of meat every day, plenty of apples in the orchard and always plenty of vegetables. We had milk puddings, rice or macaroni or sago, and plum pies or apple tarts, dishes like this, not little pie dishes like you see today! Mother used to make a fruit cake everyday and it used to get eat. Twenty Christmas puddings cooked in the boiler. We all used to have to have a stir. And she used to put money in it. I always thought that was dirty. Coins, you didn't know who might have held them!

The garden

Other domestic chores included gardening, as vegetables were needed throughout the year. Often the whole family took part in this. Any surplus could be given to neighbours and relatives. Growing flowers was a luxury, but who could resist doing that? Farm labourers would each have their own strip of ground for potatoes and so on and worked on it when they had a spare hour taking pride in their neat plots and in rivalry with their neighbours.

> *In front of the house was this massive great garden. That kept us going with everything, vegetables, fruit and flowers. She loved her garden. We all did. We all did the gardening.*

> *We bought hardly any veg. round here. You grew all your own stuff. Potatoes would be under the stairs all winter and you got spring greens and curly kale, all straight out the garden.*

> *Our orchards were all eating apples. And we used to go picking the apples and pears in, when it was time. And Mum stored them in newspaper in big boxes in part of the cellar place, like the dairy where it was always nice and cold. Potatoes would be under the stairs all winter. Mum used to make her own butter and a bit of cheese on and off and there was always plenty of milk.*

The old fashioned farmer's wife had a very important role to play in the life of the farm. The health and comfort, nourishment, and to a great extent the happiness of the family was in her hands and she was always aware of the problems of stock management and husbandry. She was queen of the house and it was her kingdom.

CHAPTER EIGHT

Services

Few communities are completely self-sufficient and this was very much the case within the valley. A rural area requires many different services to provide for the needs of its inhabitants. Within the area now covered by the lake there were farms and cottages but few other businesses and no shops or public services. All these however were available in the adjoining villages. Chew Magna was undoubtedly the business centre but each of the smaller villages provided a variety of shops and commercial business. Households usually looked to the nearest village to provide all their requirements and they only travelled further when these could not be met locally.

Transport

Over the past century the far reaching changes in transport methods and facilities did much to alter the way country people lived. In the beginning transport was very much down to the horse. If you could afford it you would have a pony and trap as your personal and family transport for visiting, for business and maybe for church going, or to shop in the nearby villages or even in town. If you had a load to carry there were various kinds of one or two axle farm carts and wagons. These were used for haulage of corn to the mill, hay to the mow, apples to the cider press, and so on. Nothing much had changed before WW1, but then the pace accelerated and by the beginning of WW2 the picture was very different. The changeover to mechanised vehicles increased, driven by the demands of the war effort and later the need to compete under the pressures of the post war period.

In the twenties and thirties very few people had a car. One farm worker remembers seeing a car for the first time going up the hill to Chew Stoke from the Villice. He said it only just made it to the top! Professionals, doctors and vets and local 'gennelmen' were the earliest owners of motor cars. At first people stared with interest but they soon got used to them. One young girl from Moreton who worked in Bristol remembered:

> *I used to wait for the bus* (on the West Harptree to Chew Stoke road, by the lane to Moreton) *and only two cars would come along and I knew which one it was by the sound. One was the doctor's car and one was the Lord of the Manor* (Charles Hill, East Harptree).

The majority of the young either walked or cycled. On leaving school and starting work many people invested all their savings in a bicycle. These did great service to get them to work, to visit friends – or even in one case to get to Bristol University! They were a source of pride and they widened horizons.

> *We used to cycle in, especially Saturdays. Sometimes we would go over Dundry Hill and down into Bristol that way and sometimes to Winford. It was quite a long journey but obviously we were quite fit in those days!*

Cycling was not without its risks, however. A young girl had a nasty accident when she toppled from her bike and was dragged by a coach along the road:

> *I never had a bone broke but I had hardly any skin left on me. I had a new dress and coat ripped to pieces that had got chewed up under the mudguard. The driver paid for a new coat and that. He was frightened to death. I rode that bike to school after that for months. When I got home from school our Mum would go up to Harptree on the bike to get her shopping with bags on the handlebars. One day I was late, she took hold of the handlebars and the bike fell all to pieces, and that was months after the accident!*

A few progressed to owning a motorbike, which reduced the travelling time and increased the distances possible. The addition of a sidecar allowed a girlfriend to be taken out and, in due course, for the wife and family to go on outings.

To begin with, a car ride would be no more than an occasional treat.

> *Of course we didn't have transport in those days. Sometimes Dad would hire Gibb's car* (with driver), *Gibb's Bishop Sutton. We used to hire the car there to take us over to Gran's but other than that we used to walk really.*

There were problems, of course, as two ladies recalled:

When we couldn't get the car to start Grandad had to go and get the horse and the cart (because the horse would kick), put it in front and tow it up over the little hill to the cross (Moreton Cross), *turn it round and run it back down again to bump start it to get Dad into Bristol.*

The first car Dad had had a dickie seat (a rear seat facing backwards) *and we had to take some geese in to Bristol. We sat in the dickie seat and one of the geese nearly got away so Dad had to get out and catch it. It was all very exciting.*

Imagine, however, the social status and advantages of acquiring your first car! Of course on a cold winter night it had to be started on a handle, the windscreen misted up, hand signals were required and it bounced and rattled down the farm road. But you kept your clothes clean and it saved all that pedalling and that mattered if you wanted to go to a dance!

Of course not everyone learned to drive. Older women were often shy of that – or perhaps the menfolk thought that they could not be trusted with the precious car. By the twenties there was a reliable bus service to Bristol but even before that there were carriers carts. The carrier had always transported goods and people from railway stations and towns to the rural communities.

There used to be someone in the village, Mr Thrush. He used to go to Pensford station delivering things and picking them up for Chew Magna.

From the middle of the 19th century networks of railway lines had developed throughout the region. At various times proposals were made to run lines close to and even through the valley but none of them were ever built. The nearest stations to the valley were at Pensford, Clutton and Blagdon; none local enough for regular public transport.

In due course the carriers moved to motorised vehicles.

Jack Shipsey at West Harptree had a lorry to take parcels in (to Bristol) *and bring parcels and goods out for people and take people in shopping. He had been doing that for a while. Luther Lyons did it but with a car. If it was reasonable parcels that you could get in the car he carried them but if it was a great bulky thing then they'd arrange for the carrier. They went to Bristol two or three times a week and you asked them to pick up things for you. And they would pick them up, bring 'em back, and you would go and fetch it from them and pay a few coppers, maybe sixpence, to the carrier.*

In several valley villages some of the carriers and owners of cars for private hire developed into bus operators.

Shipsey at West Harptree had a coach and Gibbs had one in Bishop Sutton,

Luther Lyons at East Harptree and Lyons at Blagdon. They all ran a couple of times a week into Bristol.

If any member of the family decided to go on a major shopping expedition it meant a trip to town. Of course there were drapery shops, tailors and dressmakers, and boot making was undertaken locally, but if a lady was looking for high fashion there was nowhere like a town, be it Bath, Bristol or Wells.

If they wanted to go to Bristol, my Uncle would drive my Auntie down to Fair Ash in the crank cart and she would catch the bus there and then pick her up in the evening. That was like going abroad in those days. The bus had a stop outside a shop coming out from Knowle and she said to the conductor, 'Would you go across to the shop and get me two penny'th of bullseyes?' And he did. That was to take them back you see.

Public transport was becoming more frequent and reliable and once this was established there was more confidence. Some young people relied on it to get them to the grammar schools in town and others to work. But as nowadays the service did not always suit everyone.

I used to go in by bus and the buses were on time, you could set your watch by the bus. You got to know the bus drivers and they had conductors in those days and you got to know the conductors more so than the drivers.

We used to catch the twenty to eight bus in the morning and come back on the one that left Bristol at ten past five.

Sometimes Sybil and I would go to the pictures after work but the problem was the buses back left before the end of the picture.

These private local coach firms could also be hired for regular runs or outings.

We got the contract to take the kids to the Blue School. I'd go so far as Chew Magna then all round the valley picking up kiddies and drop them at Chewton Mendip where they'd cross over the main road and get the service bus. Football teams, we took those all round the place, dart teams, table skittle teams we did take as well, evenings, you know. Then at the weekend we went on excursions, usually a long trip to Weymouth, Bournemouth or Torquay.

Blacksmiths to mechanics

In the 1930s there were still plenty of horses working on the farms and plenty of work for local blacksmiths. There were one or two in every village as well as a saddler in Chew Magna.

The last village blacksmith, Chew Stoke

We'd buy harness from anywhere. Father would go off and bring back anything we wanted – a collar or that. There was a saddler in Chew Magna, Art Veater, on the corner. One bloke used to come round and do a little bit of repairing on the farm.

The blacksmith was Spear, where the Co-Op is now in Chew Magna. I remember taking my mare to him, and of course there was Monty Ball in Winford and years ago there were two in Chew Stoke – all the villages had them. It is interesting the way some of them adapted to changing times.

Brent's at Sutton, that started as a blacksmith, then he did bicycles and gradually moved up to the motor bikes.

Blacksmiths had always made and repaired agricultural metalwork. Gradually, tractors and trailers were replacing horses and for a while the local blacksmiths were being asked to convert horse drawn implements for use behind a tractor. Shoeing horses was no longer the mainstay of their business but it was still needed.

The old Garage? It was still a blacksmith, the old shed on the side with a forge up the end and I used to dread when I heard a horse come along the road. Luther was a brilliant blacksmith. He'd buy the long lengths of iron for the shoes. He'd measure them up and then he'd put it in the fire, get that red hot, then he'd hold like a cutter chisel on there with wire tongs and I'd have to hit it with the sledge (hammer) to cut it up. And then he'd make them to shape then, punch out the holes, no drilling then, pull the horses hoof up and try it on. Of course the shoe was red hot and you could see it burn. Didn't hurt the horse 'cause they couldn't feel that but it'd blooming stink though. He'd have a look at that and then he'd trim the hoof round or do a bit more work on the shoe until he got it a perfect fit and then he'd chuck it in the trough to cool it down and then hammer it on. Anything wrought iron or that, he could heat and twist and make gates or anything. He was brilliant with that.

Luther had two petrol pumps when I started in '39 – 300 gallon tank and a 500 gallon tank. There was the cheaper sort, the two star and the three star and then it got that more grades were coming in; four star and super, 'cause Rolls Royces and Bentleys had to have a super petrol. He did have a pump with a glass container at the top, in the corner. If someone said they wanted two gallons then you would turn the handle and get two gallons up in the jar, then put the nozzle in. But then it went to electric pumps then, so that was much easier and then gradually it went on that they put the money up then.

I began to learn a little about the mechanics as well. De-coking cars, fitting new valves in the engine and all that, 'cause the valves did burn out quicker then see, because of the lead in the petrol. It's different now, do a hundred thousand miles, whereas before you could do two or three hundred, I suppose, before the cylinder wasn't working very well.

It was amazing how many cars there was about, elderly people that had them. The old Austin sixteens and eighteens, twenties and that, Wolseleys, Humbers.

Mills and 'stink factory'

There was one business, apart from farming, which had once thrived in the valley and that was milling. The history of the mills on the River Chew has already been covered in a previous chapter but the service they provided to farmers was still required until very recently.

We'd grow the crops for animal food and have it thrashed. We had a mill of our own if we wanted to grind it roughly but, if we wanted anything ground fine, like the barley ground to meal for pigs, we used to take it along to them and have it back for foodstuffs.

I used to come along to Coley Mill when it was running. When all the rest finished I took it down to Stratford Mill and Arthur Wilson. Chew Magna Mill was the very last one.

One of Arthur Wilson's daughters remembered:

As you know, my dad had a farm and then (Vowls and) *Handcock came and used the mill. I used to go out with him weekends and help him to tie the bags on at the bottom whilst he took the grain up to the hoppers to be ground. I don't think it operated every day, just when farmers brought in their things to be ground. Handcock's used to bring in lorries to haul it away and sometimes farmers took it away when they had it ground for themselves.*

On the old West Harptree to Chew Stoke road close to Ben Bridge was one other small business, the 'stink factory'. This was the local name for the building where the carcasses of dead animals which were not fit for human consumption were rendered down for fertiliser. This was an essential service in a livestock area. Many of the people we interviewed describe the appalling smell which emanated from the plant and its one-man workforce:

On the way to Chew Stoke each day on my bike I would pass the man on his way to work. Even first thing in the morning the smell was awful!

Shops and mobile businesses

Whilst Moreton itself, being a small hamlet, was too small a community and too far off the beaten track to support shops of its own there were shops of several kinds in all the neighbouring villages. Most were general stores and sold necessities in the grocery line. Others were specialists such as butchers, bakers or saddlers, or they sold hardware or drapery. However many of them recognised the importance of a delivery service to the occupiers of outlying farms and cottages and this led to the development of a network of mobile shops that is altogether remarkable in its scope and variety:

You never went shopping. It was all brought to your door years ago.

There was strong competition between these businesses and there were strong customer and family loyalties too. The Chapman family developed a shop in Bishop Sutton:

We bought the shop (Drapery shop) *in the village. Mother had been working there and it came on the market and we bought it and Olive and my Mum and myself worked that. We had everything – drapery, hardware, and footwear. We sold home perms, wellington boots, hobnailed boots, nuts and bolts, barbed wire, milk filters, strainers, anything a farmer wanted. Being in agriculture, I knew there was nowhere you could buy these things. You had to go into Bristol to get a few nails or whatever and so we started that off. We sold (shotgun) cartridges. You had to get a licence. We used to supply Potter with his humane killer cartridges. We arranged for boot repairs. We were agents for Brooks Dyeing and Cleaning in Bristol.*

A natural and enterprising development from this was a mobile round:

I started a, drapery and footwear, pay as you go, credit drapery round. You know half a crown a week or something like that. I used to do right up on the Mendips, Priddy and East and West Harptree. Not Chew Magna, they had a drapery. It was only a small seven or eight hundredweight van. A Morris 1000, I think it was. I put shelves and hangers for clothes and stuff. People would come and stand at the back. It wasn't big enough for them to get in. If it was wet, they got wet. I did more, I suppose, in the way of orders. People would say, 'Can you get me a pair of socks or a shirt for Fred?' They just asked for what they wanted.

I'd go to the warehouses in Bristol once a week with a list and restock. I'd explain what dresses were wanted and we'd go into the warehouse and look for it. Some of the stuff was on sale or return but as long as it was stock we were doing anyway, it would just go back into stock if the customer changed their mind on an order. But we did have one warehouse, a ladies, where we could get it on approval. We could go to that warehouse and pick up half a dozen dresses and take that to the customer and if they didn't want them, then we'd take them back. But we stocked dresses as well. And we used to supply a lot of stuff, not directly to the school, but we used to supply Chew Valley School uniform. We managed to get the ties and all made up.

We only sold hardware from the shop. If someone really wanted something from the shop I would take it for them next time. But I didn't carry hardware as such.

There were one or two big credit drapers companies doing rounds; Morses, Mr Kirby from Whitchurch and there was another from Chew Stoke. There were quite a few credit drapers. I think it was basically only clothes that were done on credit. There wasn't much money around. People couldn't afford to pay for things outright.

People would come in the shop too – we had a book. And they would forget to pay sometimes as well. These people were your friends and neighbours. You would drop a hint that it was about time they paid up. You didn't take people to court or anything like that. If someone owed us ten pounds, that would be a lot. It was chiefly two pound ten (shillings).

Bob Hoddinott delivering the milk

Most of the mobile businesses however, dealt in perishables. In the days before refrigerators, milk and bread were delivered daily and, if the farm was far off the road, it was common to provide a wooden box by the gate.

They used to have a little shed by the entrance to save the baker or anyone from coming all the way up to the house, he could leave it in there.

Many people obtained their milk from the nearest farm, often dropped off by a child on its way to school. Others had the regular delivery from the milkman. Certainly they never went to the shop for it.

They used to come round with milk in a churn on the back of a cart and dip out the milk into your jug.

There were many bakers who travelled throughout the area.

We had Williams from Winford because he was mother's cousin and Patch's from Regil for the same reason.

Moulder's at West Harptree did a van and Tibbs and Montgomery's at Bishop Sutton. They all did deliveries. Horse and cart originally. Montgomery's had those covered-in carts; there was a roof over the top. I

West Harptree Shop staff and delivery van, Roderick Moon centre.

think it was just before the War *they changed.*

Shops had travelling salesmen who took orders which were then delivered to their customers later in the week. A few extended their businesses by developing mobile shops. The competition between butchers is interesting. It seemed that a young wife often believed that the butcher that her family dealt with was the only one to be trusted:

> *The butcher that used to come around most of the valley was Temple Cloud butcher, Mr Chivers, and then there was a Mr Pearce at Chew Magna who came around as well and then Veater's, they started up at West Harptree. They used to cover the whole of the valley. All the different pushers used to run over the same ground. They had regular customers. You either were with Mr Veater or with Mr Chivers. And we were with Veater's.*

> *They all delivered. They would come round and they would have the meat there and they would cut the chops or whatever. Bakers were daily but I think butchers were twice a week generally. Used to come towards the beginning of the week for your chops and things and then the end of the week for your main joint. The Co-Op at Radstock, they had an outrider*

that took orders; Bill Mullins used to come round at the beginning of the week and take the order and deliver the meat Fridays. It was a really competitive market.

There were yet more suppliers. The Showering brothers came round with beer and cider in a small lorry (long before the advent of Babycham) and Mr Parsley sold oil for lamps. There was even a man who brought fish from Bristol.

There was always a fishmonger, Mr Shenton, he came from Bristol. He had a very big business. I can remember him. He always had breeches, leggings and boots and they were polished; they were so polished you could shave in those. He was so clean. And the van wouldn't have a speck of dirt on it. Every day it must have been washed.

Another surprising service was a supplier of cloth:

Material used to come round from Bristol. I used to make my own clothes. I never ordered it but if I saw something I would take it.

Our best source of information on the service provided by mobile shops has been Wilf Beer who drove one of the mobile shops for Saunders at West Harptree. He deserves to be quoted at length:

Everything and anything we used to sell. All foodstuffs, fresh vegetables, frozen, bacon, meats and that sort of thing. Anything that they wanted in drapery and all that sort of thing they could order and we would take it for them to see and, if it wasn't satisfactory, return it. We didn't do bread because there was a baker going around in those days. Not fresh fish, we only did the frozen. We had a frozen cabinet. It used to be charged up at night.

We used to go in at eight in the morning. It was a long day 'cause we never used to get back until sometimes seven o'clock at night. And it was a lot of responsibility and the weather wasn't like it is now. In the winter we used to get stuck in snowdrifts and all sorts of things like that. You used to have to drive into the farms and some of the places you had to turn round was terrible, all holes and potholes and everything.

We used to stop at most houses because they were too far apart. If we stopped where there was a rank of houses, well, then everybody came out together.

There was shelves each side and people walked up through the middle and there was a sort of counter each side for people to put their stuff on as they wanted it. They picked it up themselves, it was self-service. I stood more or less at the cab end because that was where the till and all that were. We had balance scales with weights on one side and then eventually we went into the ones which had the two sides. That was much easier. The girl used to pack it into their bags and shout and I used to write it down in the bill book and I used to add up with people talking to me!

The dried fruit went in a blue bag 'cause that was more or less waterproof – the juices wouldn't come out of it. It was special stout paper. Sugar was in the same sort of blue bags. You used to buy them by the thousand. They were already made up into bags but years ago they had to make them. Most of the tea in my time was in packets but you did still have certain loose teas. That was all done ready for us to go out, back in the shop, 'cause we couldn't have done it in the van. Cheese we used to cut on the van 'cause we had a counter that we could do that on.

I think it was mostly all supplied by a wholesaler. We didn't have a lot of local stuff. We used to do some butter. Anchor, the New Zealand butter, used to come in big lumps, 40 lbs. blocks, and then you had to cut it up into half pounds and pack it up in the paper which had 'Anchor' on it. They used to do that back at the shop so we had it all ready. Biscuits were loose, all in tins usually, and the tins used to come round with us and we'd weigh them out. And we used to do a lot of broken biscuits – tins of broken biscuits. Some people used to buy a whole tin and others we used to weigh up a pound or a half-pound, whatever they wanted.

We used to take candles and wicks and all that sort of thing for the lamps. And we took orders for paraffin and oil for lamps but that was delivered by a different van.

They did their shopping for the week off the van. Some of them used to have a bill for what they had today and pay for last week's. And if they wanted us to bring anything special the next week, then they would order it and it went on the bill.

You had to be a good supplier in those days to keep your trade. You had to put yourself out. You always talked to one another (rival firms' vans) but you had to look after your customers or they would go somewhere else.

Other services

There was certainly no lack of private enterprise in the valley. Anyone who had a skill or could identify a need might find a role. One rather unusual business was carried out by Nommy the 'Snail Man' who was well known on the Mendips and around the valley. He made his living collecting snails which he sold in Bristol for eating:

He was a nice old chap who lived rough but he was always nice and clean in himself. He showed me where to find snails in the walls and in the roots of the trees. He had these great big sacks with these tins on his back. When they were full he walked to Bristol. They must have been heavy.

Nommy the snail man would come round. He'd say to Mother, 'Can I look for snails?' He'd gently lift up the plants on the wall and look in the crevices for the snails.

There were many other services of a more conventional type available:

Bert Weaver, he was the barber in the village. He did cut everybody's hair. If you went there you were up there for the evening and it didn't matter if there were two there or fifteen. He used to have some stories.

There weren't any barber or hairdressing shops as such. There were two people in Bishop Sutton, lived side by side actually, and both their names were Harvey, no relation, and they both cut hair. Certain evenings and you just went to their house; you didn't have to book. They'd be cutting for two or three hours. Six pence or four pence I think.

I bicycled to Clutton where there was a ladies hairdresser. But home perms, of course, were very popular. Mothers or sisters would do it.

There were carpenters and general handymen. Women took in laundry while others did dressmaking and altering. This was an age when things were repaired or mended rather than thrown away and another item purchased.

There was a Mr Parfitt from Paulton who used to come round and collect boots and shoes for repair and take them back. It wasn't a shop. And Mr King at West Harptree used to do shoes. Proper shoes, that could be repaired with leather soles and hobnailed boots.

Telephones

Telephones were few and far between. It may seem strange in these days when everyone from the age of twelve upwards appears to have their own personal mobile but telephones were regarded as an extravagance and only rarely necessary.

The business people had telephones. Most people didn't have telephones. You had to go for the doctor, either cycle or walk.

There was a hand operated telephone exchange in Chew Magna and even in the 1950s you asked the operator for the number you wanted and she quite often said, 'Oh, she isn't there today, she's gone to see her sister,' or some similar gossip.

Banks and Post Offices and business

Although there were Post Offices and some kind of banking facilities in most of the villages around the valley, the main business and financial centre of the valley was in Chew Magna. There were solicitors, estate agents and auctioneers who were long established and well known to everyone. There were two medical practitioners and a dentist as well as an undertaker, everything required to service the rural community.

We always had solicitors about, actually the solicitors were mostly based in Bristol. Some people who owned land were townspeople and did business through Bristol firms.

All the business people used banks but not the general public so much. They used the Post Office. There was a bank in Bishop Sutton and of course West Harptree at one time. They only opened so many days a week. A sub-branch I suppose they called it but the main bank was obviously Chew Magna.

If capital were required by a young man determined to improve himself or by a tenant farmer preparing to buy his farm they would commonly attempt to borrow the money from a relative or old friend of the family. If this was not available it might be that someone, such as a solicitor or an Estate Manager, might well be able to suggest a person with money to invest. There were the beneficiaries of wills for instance, and sometimes the vendor himself would be willing to fund a mortgage.

Yes, they did borrow it from relatives because the banks were very loath to lend money in those days. Well, they did but money was very tight and quite often it was done through the family, or through somebody who had a bit of money and invested it, so it was all done privately.

People did have loans from a bank (to buy property). *My dad always had a bank overdraft and he always had a saying, 'If you can't pay for it, don't have it!' But that didn't apply to property obviously because you couldn't have all the money. So you had to borrow.*

A tenant on leaving, for whatever reason, would have their interests represented by one agent and the landlords by another. When negotiating the terms of a tenancy the value of in-going and out-going charges (that is to say timber on the farm, crops in the ground and unexhausted manure) were set against dilapidation and damage and that had to be negotiated. When a farm was for sale it would normally be advertised in the press and by posters and, if a sale was not agreed beforehand, it would be sold by auction, usually in a local hostelry in the early evening.

The auctioneers best known in the Chew Valley were the Kings. Edgar King was held in great respect and it should be noted that he led a deputation of farmers to the House of Commons to protest against the flooding of the valley. In the event they were not successful but he had sympathy with the farmers and helped their negotiations over the price of the land and the limited amount of compensation that the tenants received. This was a basic two years rent and was far less than would apply today.

Council services

There was no rubbish collection service in the countryside.

You had to get rid of it yourself. You burned and buried as much as you could. And everybody had a big garden in those days anyway. There weren't many tins in those days and glass was re-used. Most people had an ashes tip at the bottom of the garden, 'cause they all had fires then. And my Dad used to go round and collect that because when he built the farm buildings they were made of ashes and lime before the days of cement. He rigged up a big sieve and I remember sieving it.

Very little was wasted. Wood ash was dug into the garden anyway, as it was a good source of phosphorus. Recycling was to some extent a part of life.

There wasn't the tin cans about, not till after the War. Glass bottles were all returnable. It was mostly lemonades and squashes and things like that. We had a deposit on them.

The network of country lanes received little attention. They were muddy in winter and dusty in the summer. There were herds of cattle carrying mud from the gateways of fields to the farms. Occasionally teams of road menders filled in the potholes with crushed stones left in heaps at intervals around the valley. Another annual task was remembered:

There would be one man working for the Council and he would go round with a scythe and cut the verges. That was the only means of doing it. That would be his life. And the hedges they would grow up and they were meeting across the road.

Medical services

Provision of medical services prior to the introduction of the NHS in 1949 was very different from today. Expectations were much lower:

We never went to the hospital. We seldom went to the doctor 'cause we couldn't afford it. Not only that, we didn't get all these illnesses. I think people were fitter.

They didn't go to the doctor much but they didn't live so long.

Although people were in general healthy, due to a simple and hardworking lifestyle, when serious disease or an accident did occur then there were sometimes real problems, as there was often a delay in calling the doctor. The poorest people might delay for financial reasons and although a woman might get a doctor to her child or to her husband, the breadwinner, many women were prepared to suffer in silence themselves. Calling a doctor was an expensive option when money was short and patients would often resist taking this step until overruled by their spouse or daughter. In one family a baby who had fallen out of his pram and broken his arm near the elbow had to go to Bristol have it re-set. Later his father who suffered from a neglected prostate enlargement, and his mother who was severely diabetic, both left seeking treatment for far too long.

To a large extent there were traditional home and herbal remedies to be tried first, some of which were actually effective.

If any of us were poorly Mother used to say, 'You'd better go up to Granny Mapstone'. That was Beryl her Mother, and she used to make embrocations and that sort of thing and Mother used to say, 'Rub this lot in'. We used to wear camphor round our neck and you had to keep it on until the camphor was all gone, and we used to wear tarred string. Herbie, my brother, he used to get croup and our Mother used to get bacon fat or goose grease and rub it in his chest.

Doctors in the area are remembered with affection and respect. Between them they catered for a wide social mixture of patients. There were several practices which were eventually to grow into the present day group practices. At the southern end of the valley:

Harptree House was the doctor's house and surgery, Dr Pearson and a lady doctor who did not live locally. Later he moved the surgery to Fernlea, Old Bristol Road.

There were two in Chew Magna, Dr 'Dick' Brew and Dr Hughes. Dr Hughes was for the posh people and Dr Brew was for the others. They both had surgeries. Dr Hughes's surgery was in his house, that big house in Harford Square. Dr Brew had his surgery where it is now but it was nothing like that obviously. It was part of another building.

The following description of Dr Brew's surgery, which was in use up until the early 1960s when the two Chew Magna practices merged and the new surgery was built, gives some idea of how far general practice has come:

The facilities were dreadful. The patients did have a waiting room but they sat on long boxes with lids, which were like coffins. There was an asbestos partition dividing it from the consulting room and you could hear absolutely everything. The consulting room had poor light, no examination couch and there was no running water in the building. The doctor stood at a lectern, the patients came in, gave their notes and they stood in front, no chairs. It was a dispensing practice and there was a cider barrel (to hold water) *and the lady used to nip into the Bear and Swan with an enamel bucket and fill up that cider barrel every morning and would turn the tap on and mix up the medicines. It was all coloured liquids in those days. Patients' records were kept on an open shelf in the waiting area and the 'Dispensary' was in the consulting room.*

There was a shelf with coloured liquids and a few aspirins and codeine and kaolin poultices. They did most of the minor surgery because they had to because patients couldn't get into town. Dick Brew sewed them up without any local anaesthetic or anything.

Everything required to treat minor accidents was carried in the doctor's bag because it was just as sterile to do it in the home or, as in the following story from a retired doctor, in the field:

I was called one summer day to a farmer whose ear had caught in the swinging arm of the baler. His ear was literally hanging off. He sat down on a hay bale and I disinfected it, anaesthetised it and sewed it on. 'Oh Doctor, I hope 't's as good as t'other one that Dr Brew did. Same bloody baling machine! Mind you, 25 years ago it was different then. Dr Brew came in the field and he took from behind his lapel a needle and he picked up a stone and he rubbed the point of the needle on it to sharpen it. Then he put his hand in his pocket and took out a fishing reel and used some line to sew my ear on. Oh it hurt!'

And if you look at him you wouldn't know.

Dr Hughes had fewer but more affluent patients. His was a much more formal practice. He sent out accounts and his patients paid. But the situation was very different for the majority of people who had to pay cash for each visit to the doctor.

Generally there were Friendly Societies and clubs which people paid into – sixpence a week. Mother was in Dr Brew's club. When you were ill, he would come and that would pay him for it. So you'd paid in advance really. Nobody went to the doctor like they do today. If there was something really major they went to Bristol General Hospital.

The Friendly Societies were of great importance to working people who had no reserve to pay for urgent and unexpected medical bills. But there were other ways to pay the doctor:

Dr Dick was not good at collecting money from his patients and it seems he got a lot in kind: cauliflowers, rabbits, chickens and things like that.

Most villages had their District Nurse who was employed by the local Authority but before the NHS, patients also paid for their services. They were considerably cheaper than a doctor and so often they were the first line of medical help sought. They were all not only well trained State Registered Nurses but also Certified Midwives and they took on a lot of responsibility. They did a great deal of work but they were also often the family confidant.

1, Ridge Crescent was a council house which was always occupied by the nurse, Nurses Long and Newman. The district nurse used to travel around on a bicycle. She knew all the families.

Another contributor remembered:

Nurse... was lodging in the village. I think every village had its own nurse. She was a very hard person. She was like a man. She rode a motorbike and that was something in those days. Not many ladies rode motorbikes. Generally she dressed wounds but mostly maternity she did. She was the midwife.

Babies were generally born at home. Three of ours were born at home. I had to go to Southmead for the last one, a caesarean. In those days I don't think anyone went to hospital unless there were complications. You just got on with it. The nurse did everything, only if there were complications was the doctor called. If they needed help the doctor was there. The nurse knew when I was due and the Doctor knew and I was booked for it and he had gone off to London. The nurse was furious with the Doctor!

Not all homes had even the basic requirements for a home confinement and often neighbours were called on to help.

Nurse Newman knew how to take charge. She came to the people in the farm cottage, who were young people. Two brothers, one was married, the wife was expecting and they only had a washing up bowl, so she sends them up home and they borrowed a washbowl and jug. Another neighbour was expecting, so she went there and they only had coloured and striped towels and they were too rough for a baby, so she sent them up for my white towels. I was on the lease-lend!

So many women died in childbirth then. The National Health changed everything.

The local GPs and nurses did sterling work and earned their fee but, faced with chronic conditions such as pneumonia, tumours or arthritis, or a hundred other ailments, their weapons were very limited, particularly before the advent of sulpha drugs or antibiotics. Patients were generally nursed at home or in the home of a relative and most eventually died there. There was a dread of hospitalisation, which was associated in many peoples' minds with the Union Workhouse.

Bet Williams who lived at the cottage by Denny House Farm remembers with affection a frail old lady nearby. They did their best to help but there was only so much they could do so in the end she had to go to the Union. Another man continued hedging long into his old age. He feared a visit to hospital most:

He had to go to hospital in the end, but he wasn't in there 24 hours and then he did die. He didn't have any relatives at all. He was a dear old chap.

Very few people visited the dentist and generally it was to have teeth pulled after having severe toothache.

When we were children the Dentist used to come to the school but also there were one or two that used to come around to the house. My Mother had every one of her (teeth) out with nothing at all – no injection. Sat in the kitchen, in the chair, and had them all out. Mr Samson – a good name for a dentist. That was the general thing. The Dentist came and visited you on a certain day quite regularly. And you sat in the kitchen and he done whatever had to be done and you paid him there and then.

There was always a dentist based at Chew Magna. There was a dentist in Bristol he was called the Butcher. He was well known but everybody seemed to go to him. Maybe he was cheap!

We used to go to the Dentist on Bristol Bridge and that got bombed. Mother had been paying for to have dentures and the dentist got bombed and so she lost it (the money she had paid in) so she just went gummy the rest of her life.

There was one final service and again there would be someone from within the community to do that:

Our Mother used to lay people out. Nelson came for her to lay out his father, clean shirt, and shave and so on. She laid out Nelson's grandfather too. He lived there for about seven years and he was bedridden. He used to fall out of bed and he was a heavy man and we had to lift him back in again.

It is all too easy to find faults in the National Health Service now, but few of us, and notably the professionals, would care to return to the standards of medicine and health care in the countryside before its inception.

Police, magistrates and courts

The local policeman was well known to everyone and as most people were law abiding was more a friend than a threat, although he may have been used as such:

We (as children) *were frightened to death by the policeman. You knew your policeman and you knew what he was like. You knew that if you did something wrong and he caught you, you'd had it. There was petty crime but I mean you could leave your door open.*

There was a sergeant in Chew Magna – Sergeant Gill, a policeman in Chew Stoke, Compton Martin and (way back) East Harptree. I can't recall that Bishop Sutton had one but at Temple Cloud, which is next door up over the hill, there was a sergeant and two policemen there. That was a base station and there was one at Pensford.

There was a degree of give and take throughout the rural areas and a good policeman knew how to enlist the co-operation of the local people. It could be a solitary occupation as highlighted in the memories of a former policeman:

It was the practice in those times to have a rural police officer. I was the only one covering what was then the Compton Martin beat. This was under Frome Division and Temple Cloud was my sub-station. That sergeant there, he had a policeman at Compton Martin, one at Chew Stoke, two at Paulton, and one at Temple Cloud. That was the Temple Cloud Section. There was only one mobile vehicle attached to a section and that would be the sergeant's car. The constables that came under him had pedal cycles which were hard work when you are placed in a hilly area.

My beat would extend to Priddy, coming all the way round to East Harptree, Greendown, down to Litton and then you come on down to halfway up the hill towards Hinton Blewett and then it would come on round, take in Widcombe Common, border Bishop Sutton, to halfway over the Lake where you can turn to go up to Nempnett Thrubwell and then bordered Blagdon. And I did all that on the pedal cycle!

In those days a policeman was always on duty. He never went off duty. So I could be called out at any time. You knew what you had to do. Your work was set for the week; what you did each day, where you went, and that would show on my check. Your record was your notebook which you made up daily.

You'd do a four hours on and four hours off. So I could possibly start at ten o'clock at night with a second tour and go through to two o'clock in the morning and the only means by which they were able to contact you would be that you would be at a fixed point half way through that tour. It could be a telephone box or a house. There was one at the Castle of Comfort. So if I started duty at ten, my point at the Castle of Comfort would be at twelve o'clock. You had no means of 'phoning so if my Sergeant wanted me he had to come out and visit me there. It could take me all my time to get to the point. You didn't see a soul; there were very few cars on the road in those days.

You spent a lot of time issuing licences for the movement of animals, and for guns. At one time the policeman had to go round testing milk. Some farmers in order to increase the capacity of their milk would water it down and the policeman's job was to check it.

There was almost no crime at all on the beat. You almost made offences. Like if a person didn't sign their driving licence. That was an offence. Failing to stop at a road junction, that was a typical offence. The Magistrates Court dealt with summonses; Rees-Mogg was the Chairman, Mrs Pitt a magistrate lived at Chew Stoke. The court sat once a week and I attended as often as I could! It relieved the tedium of normal duty.

Respected members of the community were recruited as magistrates. It was a responsibility and a commitment. A former magistrate at Temple Cloud Court recalled:

When I started at Temple Cloud there were only seven of us and of course we knew everybody quite well. When we amalgamated (It closed in 1979 and amalgamated with Keynsham and Radstock.) there were 27 magistrates and then when I joined Bath there were 93! You could never get to know them all. Temple Cloud Court sat every week. As Chairman I sat once every two weeks. But you could be called at any time. It tended to be that existing magistrates would recommend new ones. They had a certain amount of training with the Clerk to the Court who came from Frome. Main cases were road traffic offences, poaching, no TV licences, and penalties for children staying away from school.

Generally they were fined but magistrates could impose sentences of up to six months imprisonment. Above that cases went to the Assizes in Wells. There were not a great many serious misdemeanours in the valley but when they did occur the scandal went from mouth to mouth and the disgrace would be very hard to live down. Reputation counted for a lot.

CHAPTER NINE

Childhood

A rural childhood for most people is looked back on as an idyllic period of innocence. We were fortunate in being able to share the reminiscences of many whose early years were spent among the fields and farmsteads of Moreton and the wider valley. Their pleasure in the fond memory of days gone by cannot be ignored. Typical are comments such as these:

I had a very happy childhood. It was a lovely place to live and there was always something going on. We had good parents and it was just all happiness.

Happy childhood? Oh God, yes, really and truly. We were free to go all across the fields. We had our chores to do, but on a Saturday when we'd done what we had to we were free. Oh yes, we had a lovely time. We didn't have luxuries but we had what mattered.

Nowadays, with the availability of pre-school, nursery, children's music, gym and dance clubs, not to mention television and computers, it is difficult to imagine how isolated the children of the Chew Valley were, even until the middle of the twentieth century.

Lack of transport dictated that most children from birth until they started school had very little contact with the wider world away from their family and immediate neighbours. Mothers remained at home to care for their children, sometimes with the help of a grandmother, but even quite modest homes might have 'a girl who came in to help mother'. Babies remained babies for a far longer period than today's young people and for some the day followed a rigid timetable of feeds and sleeps with many hours spent in their pram. Others were fed more or less on demand because, 'they be like little pigs. Give 'em a good feed and that'll put 'em quiet!'

Most families had few toys; perhaps building blocks and some picture books, others were home-made such as rag or peg dolls and carved wooden animals. Mothers and children improvised with everyday items; cooking pots, lids and spoons as musical instruments and a wooden clothes-horse with an old blanket as a playhouse. The daily activities around the home and farm with occasional trips to the nearest village shop provided the breadth of their world. It is understandable therefore that starting school at the age of five could be traumatic. Some children were so shy that the unfamiliar social interaction and the demands of school attendance exhausted them. One mother declared:

If I don't make sure to feed him as soon as he comes home it is too late, he will be fast asleep on the couch and have to be carried up to bed and he won't wake up 'til morning!

School days

At the beginning of the 20th century state elementary education was free to all with children leaving school at twelve years of age. By the 1930s the leaving age had risen to fourteen. Moreton was too small to have a school and so in practice those in Moreton and the south of the valley went to West Harptree School while those in the north part to Chew Stoke or Bishop Sutton Schools. A woman who grew up at Denny House Farm recalled:

Our address was Chew Stoke but we went to church in Sutton, to school, Sunday school, and the shops. Chew Stoke wouldn't have been much farther but of course it was very hilly. Sutton was a nice level walk.

But the children living in Moreton, just a mile south, headed in a different direction:

Although we were in the Parish of Compton Martin we looked to West Harptree for everything. Compton Martin was a little bit further away, you see. So we went to West Harptree School.

We walked to West Harptree. We always used to reckon it was about two and a half miles but it probably wasn't as long as that. Anyway, it seemed quite a long way. We used to meet up with other families from Moreton and go up together. If it was pouring with rain Dad used to take us up on

West Harptree School c1930: (back row) George Salvidge, John Patch, Jack Fry, Walter Weeks, Walter Goldstone. (row 2) Dennis Tucker, Vera Miles, Violet Veater, Dorothy Tucker, ? Mary Chappel, Margaret Branch, Dora Maggs, ? , Jimmy Redman, (row 3) Christine Smart, Lily ? , Maisy Noakes, Christine Tooze, ? , ? , ? Baber. (front row) Gerald Farrow, Gordon Harper, Harold Taviner.

the pony and trap and we used to travel under a big tarpaulin. It was a bit claustrophobic but we didn't get wet. On the first day Mum would take us and then we would go up by ourselves afterwards. I remember when my sister went, she's five years younger than me, we took her up and she was missing halfway through the morning. She had walked back home. She didn't like it but she was all right next day.

The villages' primary schools although small were usually divided into two or three classes with numbers as high as 40 in each mixed age class. The curriculum followed still placed a high emphasis on the 'three Rs' – reading, writing and arithmetic with additional classes in nature studies and geography and history, both of which concentrated on the British Isles and its Empire. The history and geography textbooks would be seen as prejudiced and very racist nowadays. Post-eleven boys would learn gardening and woodwork while the girls learned cookery and home-making skills. In some village schools before 1930 older boys who had 'done all the books' might be sent out to dig or hoe the schoolmaster's garden or help his wife to hang her washing! They could leave well before their fourteenth birthday and 'be out in the ground ploughing with hosses the next day'. The following quotations refer to different schools around the valley:

> *There were two classes, the Infants and then the other class. The big classroom was divided in two with a curtain – so you had the top grades and the bottom grades. Mind you it could be a bit difficult at times. The curtain was there but when they were chanting down that end it could take you off a bit. They would insist on mental arithmetic, things you had to be quick at and things that you really used. And times tables were learned by rote.*

> *All the age groups mixed very happily, no problems at all. I used to like English and Geography. I learnt to knit and sew and crochet and obviously we didn't have any cookery because it was wartime. I think the boys did woodwork.*

> *I would say it was a wonderful school because we learnt things they don't learn now. We had a teacher Dorothy Andrews. When we were kids we didn't appreciate how dedicated they were.*

> *Miss Harris was the infant teacher, she was lovely. She used to cycle from Stowey. In those days there would be a third of a pint bottle of milk. They had the great cast iron tortoise stove, which burned coke, in the middle of the classroom and in the wintertime she would always put all our milk into a big saucepan and she would warm it up. That was all the drink we used to get during the day.*
> *Then of course there was Miss Rossiter, she used to be the headmistress and during the war we used to have a lot of different teachers 'cause they used to come down from London with the evacuees.*

> *You carried your lunch and just ate it anywhere. There was a little area at the front and another one at the back and then we had a field where we could go for sports – up round the back of Moulder's. We went there once a week and went through drill.*

Discipline was strictly imposed with punishments ranging from standing in the corner, being kept in after school to writing lines or, the ultimate punishment; the cane.

> *We had a head teacher I didn't think much of. He was very strict. Oh, I had the cane, I don't know how many times.*

There was no secondary school in the area and only a few valley children on reaching eleven and the end of their primary education passed the examinations enabling them to go on to grammar school. In most schools it was known that the head teacher would identify the brighter children as soon as they reached the junior class and would begin to groom them for the scholarship two years before they were due to take it. In 1935 one boy who had attended Chew Stoke Primary School gained a scholarship to Bristol Cathedral School. His father was a miner at Bromley Colliery.

I used to go in by bus. It was a bit of a change for a country boy with working class parents. We had to manage to get the uniform and books together. I felt a bit of a twerp, I was used to shorts and they put me in a black coat and pinstripe trousers and I was only that high. My parents had to make sacrifices but we survived.

And a woman from Moreton who had gone to West Harptree School remembered:

I passed my 'eleven plus' and I went to Wells Blue School then and to start with it wasn't for the better.

Luther Lyon's coach picked me up and took me to Chewton Mendip where we caught the service bus with all the ones that came from Clutton and Farrington Gurney.

I was the only one from Moreton. I was amongst people who were sons and daughters of professional people. Being a farmer then wasn't the best thing – you were more a gypsy type.

The social strata in those days were much more clearly defined.
There were several private schools in the valley, Newton House at West Harptree and Sacred Heart at Chew Stoke which were attended by the better off families in the area. Several families sent their children to the local village primary school and then at the age of eleven they moved to Sacred Heart or Wells Cathedral and some even boarded at schools further away.

The 1944 Education Act raised the leaving age to fifteen and recognised that all children should be provided with free secondary education. At eleven children were all to leave primary school and be 'selected' to attend a grammar school to follow an academic curriculum, or a modern secondary with a practical bias. However, in the Chew Valley the provision for secondary education was very different as a former teacher remembered:

This area of north Somerset was the last area in Somerset to be reorganised; with the result Chew Magna School was from five to fourteen and then rose to fifteen. We had at one stage in that school well over 200 children.

*The valley had two All Age Schools, Chew Magna and Bishop Sutton;
they took the 'big ones'. The children from the Harptree end (primaries)
went to Bishop Sutton All Age. Chew Magna took the children from Chew
Magna, Chew Stoke, Winford, Regil, and Dundry Primaries. About three
buses would come in and out, hence our numbers. We had two classes
upstairs in the Old School Room at Chew Magna; between them was a
wooden partition on wheels, which was moved out and put away.*

*There was the Infants class, the Primary class and then there was first
year, second year, third year and fourth year. And each year was 35 to 40
mixed boys and girls. I started with the first years and gradually moved up
to the top class. I had these youngsters in this one room from nine o'clock
until four with a lunch break when we went over to the Church Hall where
the lunches were cooked. There were no laboratories, no languages, no
workshops, and no cooking. There was one break in the week, Monday
morning, when the boys in the top two forms went to Bishop Sutton for
woodwork and the girls spent the morning at Pensford School doing
cooking. The workshop at Bishop Sutton was in the Village Hall and they
had to assemble their collapsible workbenches.*

*During the War there were very few men in these schools. They had no
games until I arrived. I had come from a situation where discipline was
something and the children responded. I started doing PE Service style.*
(He had been a pilot instructor during the War.)

*Only the bright children were entered for the 'eleven plus' and they were
coached on. From Chew Magna they went to Bristol but there were very
few places. The County paid for some places at Colston's Boys School and
Merrywood.*

*We were the last area in the County to get a new secondary modern –
we were furthest from Taunton. Nobody bothered much about us up here.
We were truly rural and there wasn't the political push from the rural
community.*

*The land for Chew Valley School was bought in 1935 and it should have
been built. But the War came and post War we were the last. In 1958 we
opened and we then took Chew Magna All Age, Bishop Sutton and
Pensford All Age which was a smaller school. All the staff from the three
schools was offered a job at the new school.*

In 1908 school meals, milk and medical examinations for children had been
introduced.

The idea was for everybody to have it (medical examinations) *but the facilities weren't there and particularly in rural areas there was a load of suspicion. 'This is interfering with families – trying to take my kid away from me!' Yes, school milk went to all children but of course they were giving TB as well.* (Introduced through unpasteurized milk.)

By the end of the Second War they were doing routine school medical examinations at least once a year. The Local Authority employed doctors to do school medicals. There was a Dr Gordon at Chew Stoke who used to do it but nurses did a lot as well.

Home life

By modern standards conditions at home were primitive, almost all houses being cold and damp unless good fires were kept. Most shared a bedroom with siblings or another member of the family; oftentimes even a bed.

I shared the bedroom with my grandfather. There was a big curtain, a brown curtain with a frieze at the top in blues and golds, around my bed and the window.

We didn't have a bathroom, we had one of those long tin baths, I would be at one end our Mike at the other; our Mum didn't waste any water! We'd say Mum the water's getting cold, and she'd get the kettle of boiling water and pour it in. She didn't say stand up and let me pour it in, she'd just pour it in and if you didn't scramble out of the way you'd get burnt. We used to have some fun. Friday night it was bath night, have your toenails cut and have your syrup of figs.

Babies and toddlers were dressed in hand-knitted or sewn garments, usually white, while children were dressed like little adults. Girls wore dresses or skirts and blouses or sweaters. Boys wore shirts and pullovers like their father but with shorts until they left school. Many items would be home-made or cut down from other garments.

I was quite a tomboyish girl. There were no feminine things, you see, but I didn't have any trousers. I was in skirts but I could wear shorts. Granny used to knit my sweaters.

Many mothers took great pride in dressing their children smartly for church and special occasions. A woman with two sisters remembered:

She always used to have us the same. Lots of people used to comment on the fact how well we were turned out. One I remember; we each had a suit, we called it a three piece in those days – it was a dark blue, a pleated skirt, a little jacket and a little velvet tam-o'-shanter to match.

Children were expected to help in the home and on the farm with many having their chores to do before and after school.

In the morning before I went to school I always had to make sure there was enough stick and wood and coal in to keep the fires going. My job in the summer, when the milking was finished, was to take the cows up to the fields on my way to school and that was always interfering with my school time. If they hadn't finished then I was late for school. I was not the only pupil to do this chore but I was the furthest away, over two miles from the school in West Harptree. On the way home I brought the cows back to the farm for milking. I would help get the tea and help Mother with the cleaning up of the milk buckets and things. She must have done it with the big kettles from the kitchen. One of my jobs was to take the empty milk churns, two or three, back up into the farm.

We all had our jobs to do. One had to make the beds, one had to get the lighting stick, one to clean the boots, fill up the oil lamps, and pump the water.

I had to get up and milk five cows before I went to school. They were in the shed.

As a child I had to milk one cow before I went to school. That was my job. And run round, lift up the hatches and let the hens out and then my parents would feed them. Then I'd rush round and shut them in again at night and milk this one cow. I suppose it would take me probably twenty minutes to milk a cow 'cause my arms weren't very strong and I always thought I had the hardest cow to milk anyway. I used to get a ha'penny a day. (That would be considered good pocket money in those days.) *I used to spend half an hour looking in the sweet shop window to spend that ha'penny and try an' get as much as I could for it.*

Even outside of farming families children would be expected to help their parents, especially where, to make ends meet, their father took on another job:

My father was a miner at a local pit but he also had another job he was sexton/verger at the Church. I used to have to help him. I remember one thing sticks out in my mind very vividly. I may have been only about twelve or thirteen at the time. We used to have to light the furnace in the winter on the Saturday morning. He would bank it in before going home to lunch and then he would go on to work later on in the night. And I'd to go up there about eight o'clock and put coke on and adjust the air supply and that used to frighten me to death; creeping across the churchyard in the dark with all these tombstones all round about me, deathly silence. I always had the feeling that someone was going to jump on my back. Then I had to make my way below the church down some steps into a very dark furnace room and I used to close the door and make the necessary adjustments. I always had the feeling that the door was going to open and someone was going to put their head round. It was very, very frightening. I was glad to get home.

We had to keep the church absolutely clean. We had oil lamps in those days and they had to be cleaned and supplied with oil and all that. Father's job also involved general maintenance and he also dug a few graves in his time and was responsible for the upkeep of the churchyard. He used to cut the churchyard twice a year. We didn't have machines, we just had sickles and scythes and clippers. We boys had to help. He couldn't have managed on his own.

Children rarely received pocket money but when they did it was quickly spent.

The only time I went to West Harptree was with my brother to the sweet shop on the corner. And we used to run there because on a Saturday we got a ha'penny and he used to have coconut chips and we'd have a pointed bag, the old fashioned sweet bag.

Many children often earned small sums by doing jobs for neighbours.

We didn't get pocket money regularly. My friend, Sybil, her dad had the baker's shop and sweet shop, Moulder's in West Harptree, and I used to help there sometimes.

I had to get my own money. From about nine, I was working for Mrs Holbrook at Herons Green Farm on a Saturday for half a crown a week. I had to clean the house.

Apparently there was always room for enterprise and initiative as the following quotations illustrate:

As a child I always done the poultry, hens and ducks. I used to go down the river and collect the wild duck eggs, bring them back, hatch them out and cross them with the runner ducks. I had great fun with poultry. I used to do this for Mother really. It was more or less a woman's pin money then.

Oh, and primroses! Grove field was a very small field. The farm was named after this little field which wasn't even attached to the farm. If you went down to Grove field you could get baskets and baskets of primroses which I sold to Mr White in Stoke Villice who had a butcher's shop in Bedminster, Bristol. I used to take all these hips and haws and primroses and blue bells. I kept him going. I had thruppence a bunch. Mind you, they had to be big bunches with lots of leaves coming out.

Down at Walley Court there was the daffodil ground and we used to pick daffodils and primroses to sell during the War.

We picked blackberries and rose hips to take to the school and we got money for them. And we picked primroses to sell. We had to give over the money but we got it back to go to Harvest Home.

It seems that even this came under parental control!

Play

Once school was finished and the chores completed their time was their own. With no television or computer most of their free time was spent outside. Unlike the children nowadays they could wander freely with few restrictions, although that is not to say that there was no concern at all:

I was always told to keep away from the big bull tied up. And when the bull was out in the yard with the cows, I was banned indoors, always. 'Why can't I go out Mum?'

In general though, as the children became older, there were many simple pastimes to be enjoyed. Many of the people we interviewed had vivid memories of the happy times in their childhood:

Ours was a very idyllic childhood really. We were allowed to go anywhere we wanted to. We all had bikes. We used to have our spinning tops and our hoops, which we used to play on the way to school. Obviously we had our dolls but I was a little bit of a tomboy really. I climbed trees like an ape. You never stayed indoors and sat around, we were always out doing something. It was a very active life. As long as we were back in time for our meals and Mum knew where we were going, we had complete freedom. It was wonderful.

For us kids we had a beautiful life. I knew every inch of that wood out there and the river of course, fishing. It was terrific for kids. I used to fish in the river Chew when I was younger. I never fly-fished, we used to use what we called 'dead lines'. We never had a rod but we got the proper tackle and a cork for a float with a worm on the hook and chuck it in. We were sitting out on the bank fishing out Byemills one day. There were notices up 'Chew Valley Fly-Fishing Club'. We never took any notice of that and these two guys come along the other side of the bank and said, 'You know you're poaching. This is our water'. And my mate Oldie said, taking the mickey, 'No it's not. It only came down last night; we had a heavy storm'. They couldn't do very much; it was too deep to get at us.

As a boy I used to know every nook and cranny of the lanes in the valley. Of course we used to cycle a lot in those days.

We played in the fields. We played cricket and football and we used to look for mushrooms in the fields and blackberries and hazelnuts and we used to get filberts for Christmas. And it was great fun. Scrumping for apples; I have been chased out of orchards many, many times. The orchard I remember was Mr. Keel's. Denny Farm had a field of rather nice mushrooms there. There was one farmer in Chew Stoke if you were out picking mushrooms he would get out his gun and fire it over your head.

No TV then. All we had was a wireless. You had to accept what your parents wanted so we used to spend an awful lot out of doors; playing cricket and football and playing hop scotch, marbles or conkers and going for walks around the fields getting wild flowers, getting sticks for the fire. We had coal fires in those days and they had to be lit everyday. We used to go fishing for trout using our fingers. I used to go with someone who was very good at that. We had great fun.

We used to follow the stream round from Chew Stoke and that would connect up with the river Chew. We would start here and work all round looking for birds, moorhens, water rats and things like that. We would come out by Ben Bridge and the smelly factory; the Stink factory we called it. Oh, it was horrible. So we had that round trip. We collected eggs for our collections. That was quite acceptable in those days because there was plenty of wildlife then, sparrows, blackbirds, thrushes they were everywhere. Moorhen's eggs you could eat but we didn't. Moorhens might have a dozen eggs and pigeons always had two. I remember seeing an owl's nest once and there were two owl chicks and they were absolutely beautiful.

And us girls we used to have a big swing on this big conker tree and we used to swing and jump off and jump into the big millpond at the side of the mill. I wasn't a good swimmer but the other girls were and they always rescued me. Someone would be in the water while one jumped. It was great fun really.

In the hot weather I used to invite Jean Tibbs from Bishop Sutton School down after school and we'd paddle in the stream. Some of the Bishop Sutton lads would come and swim.

I was never lonely; I had the animals. I was friends with Pam Tucker from about the time of me being eight or nine. Each of us had to do our chores before we could meet up. I had all my hobbies outside. I kept all my flowers and all my birds nests and all my sticklebacks and minnows that I brought back.

But children left to entertain themselves for too long sometimes get up to mischief as one Moreton woman remembered:

I let all that water out of there (mill pond) one day. I was being naughty. I went into the building and turned this...and let the water out. I let the lot down across the fields. I thought our cows looked a bit thirsty so I sent some water. I was about eight or nine. I was always getting into trouble. You were neglected as a child. I did have two younger brothers but I had to be mother to them. But when I could get away, I would get up to all sorts of mischief. I never owned up to doing it.

Scrumping apples – I had the biggest orchards of our own at my disposal. So why did I go and pinch other people's? My job was to get the stick for the fires and I would always take other people's stick, not ours. I sold all my grandfather's holly and mistletoe to Bert Clark who took our full milk churns away in the milk lorry from Mendip Dairies, Chew Stoke. He was a great mate of mine. Of course he was – he was doing very nicely out of me. I got a whack of money on that. I had to give back all my money to grandfather. He would have got more at the Fat Stock market!

We used to put tins on the wheel (Stratford Mill wheel) *to see whose tin would stay on the longest. Art Wilson would chase us off. It was just a bit of fun, nothing nasty.*

At home, at church and at school children were taught discipline, respect and manners. Naughtiness and disrespect were punished, often by being sent to bed and sometimes with a spanking. Manners and respect were expected towards their 'elders and betters'.

We did never quarrel. If we had we'd a had to go to bed. If we didn't behave ourselves we got a good hiding.

Of course we were brought up that everybody was Mr and Mrs; no first name calling for us.

Chew Magna Boy Scout Troop with Den Chubb, Walt Wyatt, John Birkett, Alan Lyons, John Taviner, Norman Dury, Alan Griffin.

Organised activities

There were some organised activities. There were football and cricket teams in most of the valley villages but there were no junior sections and so although they played among themselves they didn't join clubs until they reached their teens. After the age of eleven they were eligible to join the Young Farmers, though this tended to attract the children of farming families. There were Boy Scout troops at Bishop Sutton and Chew Magna and later Harptree and there were Girl Guides in Chew Magna. But for most children living in the Chew Valley, the distance from home meant few attended. Some children however learned to play an instrument and some went to dancing classes.

Mrs Hughes, she ran the Guides. Once Mrs Hughes took three of us to Ireland camping. Myself and Betty Arthur and Nita Wedlake and we made the front page of 'The Guider'. It was 1934 when Mrs Hughes stopped.

We used to have dancing classes, tap-dancing and ballet dance in the hall (West Harptree). I believe the teacher was a Miss Jones who came out from Bristol. I paid a few pence. I rather liked it. My sisters didn't go.

Mrs Veater, the butcher's wife, in the village (West Harptree) taught the piano. But I didn't do anything with it. I regret it now to be honest. The problem was Brenda my sister could play anything by ear. She'd hear it once and she could play it and she was marvellous. I didn't get much chance to practise.

Boys too learned to play:

We had music lessons. I had a couple of years on the piano. Music teachers used to come into the village and teach. She would go to the house so you had to have your own piano. Miss used to walk all the way from Clutton to Bishop Sutton. I suppose she would do two or three of an evening.

Apart from school the main organised activity for children revolved around the church. Again there was no church in the valley and so families usually went to their nearest village church. This applied to children from most backgrounds, farmers, miners, and all other country callings.

On Sunday we went to church three times a day: morning; Sunday school and six o'clock service, evensong.

A woman living towards the north of the valley recalled:

Mother used to send us all to Sunday school at Chew Stoke.

But from Stratford Mill:

We went to church at West Harptree. All us girls were in the choir. We all went to Sunday school. We had to, strict orders. Mum and Dad were very Christian people. We were always brought up to be good mannered and do as we were told to do. We didn't get away with anything then.

While someone from Moreton recalled:

We were in the church choir; all four of us were in the choir as kids. We used to go to choir in the morning, matins at eleven, Sunday school in the afternoon and then evensong at night. We used to go four times on a Sunday we did.

One man who was in Chew Stoke Church Choir for 65 years remembered carol singing around the neighbourhood:

That was how we got paid, you see. We used to start out on Boxing Day about nine o'clock and we'd sing carols at all the houses in the village where we'd expect to get some money. We used to start off at the Rectory. We handed in a book, he gave us a pound and he put a pound in the book and his signature. Then we would have to go to the next one and the next one. Woodford House, Mr Conway lived there, we used to get ten bob (ten shillings or 50 pence) there. That was a lot of money in those days. It was a long way to go down there to get it, but it was worth it to get ten shillings. And we would go all round the village and were singing from about nine o'clock in the morning until about seven o'clock at night. We sang the carols so many times we didn't need any sheets; we knew them off by heart. The book was a record of all we had collected and then at the end the choirmaster would add it all up. And he'd have a record of all the attendances, Sunday and practise attendances. And he'd divide it all up in accordance with the number of attendances you'd put in during the year.

This was a ritual. It must have gone on for many, many years. That stopped soon after the War. It wasn't resurrected in the same manner.

Sometimes we got invited in and we got apples and chocolates and things like that. The bell ringers used to do the same. To get their reward they'd do the same as us but get the handbells out and play tunes. They'd be about half an hour ahead of us. Of course they got invited in and it wasn't apples and chocolates for them, it was something a bit stronger.

The churches were well attended and they often also provided the main social activities for the whole family. Most churches had junior choirs. Sunday schools were popular and very well attended. The Methodist Sunday school at Bishop Sutton was particularly popular, with children of all denominations travelling there from several miles around.

The highlight of the year was the annual Sunday school outing. Going on the trip entailed either regular attendance at Sunday school with details being recorded in a little book or the payment each week of a small sum of money. Most trips included the whole family and everyone would wear their Sunday best. Up until WW1 outings would have been a farm wagon ride to a field for sports and a picnic tea. But by the 1920s the outing was almost always to Weston-Super-Mare, which gave most families their only trip to the seaside and possibly their only outing together all year.

As a family we never had a holiday. I don't think Mum had a holiday in her life. But there was the Sunday school outing in a charabanc to Weston. We would get down on the sand as quickly as possible.

We had a Sunday school outing. I think that was every other year to Weston-Super-Mare. We went by charabanc, about three charabancs. The whole family went. I think the parents paid but not the Sunday school children. It didn't take as long as it does now. The roads were empty. You could have a clear run.

We thought Weston was wonderful because when we arrived at eleven or so the tide was always in but what we didn't realise was that that day was specially chosen. We weren't the only ones. The sand was divided into sections. St Andrews Chew Stoke would be here with flags at the boundary and then there would be other ones from other villages. They all knew when the tide would be in at midday. It was a very good idea because you all concentrated in one area so if anyone wanted to find someone they'd go to that spot.

I remember a traumatic experience on one occasion. I got lost. Mother was very keen on shopping but she didn't get the opportunity very often and so at Weston she was in and out of the shops all the time. And I lost her. I was six years of age at the time. I was crying my eyes out and some kindly policeman came along, put his hand on my shoulder and said, 'Sonny, what's wrong?'

I said, 'I've lost me mother'.

'Alright, where you come from?'

I said, 'Chew Stoke'.

'Oh, that's not very far.' He thought I'd said Kew Stoke, just up the hill. So he took me along to the police station and Mother collected me about an hour later. But I cried and cried.

The other year we would have a Christmas party in the hall, the Hut (Chew Stoke), *which is now pulled down, and that was exciting too. We would have a whacking great Christmas tree and each of us would have a present and we used to wander round the Christmas tree and see if we could identify our parcel. We had party games, musical chairs and things like that, and we always had jelly and cream for tea.*

For children Christmas has always been an exciting time. But in the first half of the 20th century the emphasis was far less on the commercial aspect and much more on it being an important religious festival and family occasion. After church in the morning many of the people we interviewed remembered family arriving or going to visit other relations. It was one of the few days in the year when agricultural families, living on different farms, had the opportunity to get together. They remembered the Christmas dinner, playing games and singing together and often at the end of the day sharing a bed with cousins.

We had a wonderful time, especially at Christmas time. We didn't get much in our stocking but Christmas was absolutely magic. I'd get a few sweets, an orange and an apple, and nuts and perhaps a small toy or something. Magic.

We never had much. Only at Christmas we used to have one big toy between us. We didn't have things like they do now.

The pattern of the seasons and the farming year determined many activities from picking primroses to sell, to helping with the harvest. All villages had a summer fete, some had flower shows and some a harvest supper but few villages had an event the scale of Chew Stoke Harvest Home. Pocket money was saved all year to be spent at the fair and children eagerly prepared for the competitions.

The Harvest Home we looked forward to for weeks and weeks on end, saving up our money. They had a fun fair then the dodgems and the roundabouts. Just the one day but they come in on the Wednesday or Thursday from Mark to start erecting and they'd be gone on the Sunday.

The children showed wild flowers and handwriting and catching the 'most white butterflies' was another one. White butterflies eat cabbages and they wanted them dead to stop them eating their cabbages. I got 600 one year. I counted them and brought them in a large jar. It had on the side '600' but they didn't bother counting them. They took my word for it but I got five shillings and that was a lot of money. I found the best way to catch them was to get an old tennis racket. They don't fly straight. It was a heck of a job!

Someone else also remembered entering the same competition:

At Chew Stoke Harvest Home I always entered the number of white butterflies. I never won. The girl that always won had a whacking great card and them all pinned on one at a time looking absolutely wonderful. I'd jam them into a jam jar. Nobody could tell how many I had. They'd break... bits everywhere.

Birthdays were marked each year but only the better off families would hold a children's party. 'May Curry over in Moreton Farm, we would go to one another's birthday parties.' The range of friends available was perhaps restricted but they came from a background that was similar and that was what mattered.

By the time children had reached twelve they were beginning to join in with adult social activities. They would attend church socials and whist drives. Local dances were often family occasions and in most of the village halls there would be film shows and sometimes pantomimes and variety shows.

Leaving school

On leaving school, boys and girls had to earn their living and so find work. Not many families could afford to support them and therefore further education was out of the question even if they wanted it. Few young people in rural areas without further education had ambitions beyond finding a job locally. Some boys found apprenticeships in trades or work in shops but the majority went into agricultural work with most expecting to work alongside their fathers.

> *I think I always felt I would be following Father's footsteps. I remember my Dad saying, 'Do you want to come and work on the farm or would you like to go to college and learn a bit more?' And I didn't like school anyway. I said, 'No, I'll start work'. I suppose education then wasn't as important as it is now. We had less opportunities really.*

The eldest daughter on a farm would often remain at home to help in the dairy and around the home.

> *Shall I tell you what happened? I was told my place was on the farm. You didn't have a choice in those days. I wanted to be a nurse. You just did what you were told. I left school at fourteen and a half. I worked out on the farm. My brothers worked on the farm too, they didn't do anything indoors. They didn't in those days; they never picked up a cup and saucer off the table. I never thought about that. Mother ran the house she had to feed the family and the workers. I got up about six o'clock. In wintertime you finished when it was dark. It was all right, just a way of life I suppose.*

For many girls service in a private house was still a major source of employment.

> *People haven't got maids now. Skivvies as they used to call them. I used to work all hours because you had to do evening meals. We got one half day a week and alternate Sundays half day, and one full day a month off. They wouldn't do it today. I was a maid, parlour maid. I had to get the table laid and see the meals were served.*
>
> *I earned about £36 a year. That didn't work out very much, did it? Course you got your food and lodgings. You had to provide your own uniform. What my Mother got wasn't suitable for her (employer). So she said if I stayed six months she would provide a uniform.*

Although one young girl was under pressure from her family to become a nurse she nevertheless chose domestic work:

I left at fourteen and went into service. I wanted that. I went to Dr. Hughes. They were a good family.

But by the 1930s the opportunities for girls had improved slightly. While many still went into service others went into shops or with the improvement in public transport into secretarial work. A major employer was Fry's Chocolate Factory at Keynsham who provided transport and paid very well. However for all girls the ambition and expectation was marriage and a family.

You didn't have much choice. I had this job promised to me (through family contacts) *when I left school in J P Sturge. So from my point of view things were very simple really. My friend Sybil came to J P Sturge with me. I wanted to be a hairdresser really!*

For the woman who had passed her 'eleven plus' and attended the Blue School her education may have opened up her horizons but her hopes were to be dashed:

I had a great ambition to be a vet but the money wasn't there. I only stayed until the fifth year (age sixteen). I was called in front of the headmistress when it was time to start making plans. Mother was called down and she had a long conversation with the headmistress. I was kept outside the door and then I was invited in and asked what I wanted to do. 'I want to be a vet.' There was a long silence and then the headmistress said, 'Well, I've spoken to your mother about this and there is no money. We have decided that you will go to commercial college for a year because we understand that girls of your age will get married and your mother has informed us that your two brothers need four year apprenticeships.' And they did. They had them. You did what you were told.

So when I finished at Wells I was put into commercial college and learned shorthand and typing. The alternative (to the Blue School, Wells) would have been Bishop Sutton School. Many of the girls left there and went on to Fry's and earned double the money I could get.

On the other hand the miner's son who went to Bristol Cathedral School was able to go on to university in due course. Much depended on parental backing. They may have left school and now be working but the majority of young people were still living at home under the authority of their parents. Each week they handed their pay over to their mother and received some pocket money in return. Independence was still a long way off. Gradually they would take on more responsibilities, make new friends and do more away from their families. Much was to change in the war years. But for many their twenty-first birthday literally meant receiving the 'key to the door'. Not until they married and left home were they fully independent and considered to be adults.

CHAPTER TEN

Social Life and Entertainment

The concept of leisure time was unfamiliar to most people living during the first half of the 20th century. Those employed away from the land worked five days with a half-day on Saturday and until 1938 and the Holidays with Pay Act very few workers had paid leave. All they were entitled to were the statutory public holidays and these were far less than we have nowadays. Gradually from the 1930s, more and more workers began to enjoy the benefits of a shorter working day and week. At the same time higher wages and the availability of labour saving devices gave people the opportunity and time to enjoy leisure pursuits such as home entertainment, hobbies, games and sport.

Activities at home.

For those who made their living from farming the working day was long and physically hard. Agricultural labourers worked six days a week with the hours frequently depending on the season and weather. Farmers and housewives rarely had a day off and their social life was often part and parcel of the working week. Farmers looked forward to market day and would regularly stop to chat with a neighbour on the road.

Sunday was the only time you were free. We used to go and do the milking, come home about nine o'clock, have some breakfast and then we were free 'til half past three, milking time in the afternoon.

For many the working day was determined by the length of daylight. It would still be true to say of the residents of the Chew Valley, whose homes were mostly lit only by oil lamps, that they rose with the dawn and went to bed soon after dark. Much of life was taken up with a busy routine of everyday tasks and seasonal demands. When needed every member of a family worked for long hours and expected to do so. Most women felt that they could not sit down or relax whilst there was still work to be done and certainly not before their partner had completed his own farm chores. On the other hand there were activities that could be part of home life. Mending was essential but sewing and embroidery could enhance the home with rag rugs, patchwork quilts, tablecloths and mats. Many women and girls sewed and knitted their own clothes and clothes for the children.

> *Of course there was no television in those days. I used to do a lot of sewing in the evenings. Traycloths and tablecloths and the like. I made all my own clothes and I used to make clothes for other people sometimes. I had a sewing machine. And I did loads of knitting.*

It could be argued that she was usefully employed. Many people took pleasure in gardening as a family activity, children might have their own little plot, and herbs and flowers were tended when there were no more pressing tasks to be attended to. Some people were readers but even this could be considered counterproductive. One woman actually said:

> *I used to go to the library van but I had to put a stop to that because when I had a nice book I used to spend too much time reading. I wouldn't be able to put it down and I didn't get my work done.*

These were the early days of wireless broadcasting and that made a big difference to country people. By 1922 there were regular Home Service News broadcasts which were the main source of information, although filtered during wartime by government censorship. Then:

> *The Light Programme provided popular music. I remember when wireless came first and people said, 'You can even do ironing and listen to music'.*

Not everyone approved. In one family of strict chapel goers, when the cricket commentary was followed by a programme of dance music the mother would immediately come in and turn it off. She thought it would be a bad influence on her young sons! But that was not the general reaction.

> *We used to go up to Cobb's at Pensford and get the accumulators for the wireless. We had two; one would be charging and the other we'd be using. It would only last about a week. The wireless was on every night. No telly then!*

Where there was the least interest in music the family would gather round the piano to play and sing and everyone had their song or piece of music.

My sister was a very clever pianist and we used to have lovely parties round the piano in the sitting room.

Sheet music was popular through the twenties and thirties and most homes had a wind up gramophone and a few records. For some, music was an integral part of everyday life. One of our informants painted a touching picture of a family scene:

Dad used to sing to us – real old songs. He had a lovely voice and he'd come home from the pit and have a bath and have his meal and then we'd sit on his lap and we'd brush his hair. We had a thing about brushing his hair. It's a wonder he had any left. And he'd sing to us and his eyes would be closing because he'd be ready to go to bed.

My Dad played the piano, the piano accordion, mouth organ, concertina, and everything by ear. He could play any instrument at all. Everything except the fiddle.

There were of course visits by relatives, family ties being strong and valuable both socially and when practical help was needed. With brothers and sisters, daughters and sons married or working on other farms, occasions such as Christmas, weddings, christenings and funerals were an important and rare opportunity to gather together, catch up on news and enjoy each other's company.

Cider

Cider was another traditional part of life in this valley as in most parts of the West Country. In some farming families where there was a quantity of cider made for home consumption or for sale there were naturally, tasting sessions. Card parties were much enjoyed. The following account is fairly typical:

Father-in-law made cider to sell. He kept about ten or twelve barrels at the back of his main house for special. He'd say, 'Come on, let's taste this'. And of course he would have the cup and we'd go round and taste a dozen barrels. And then we used to go in, and he always had a lot of company there, and we'd sit down and play Farmer's Glory – a card game for highest stakes mind. I've never played it since! He'd have a gallon jug (earthenware) on the table, and there would be eight of us round the table playing, and he would have his pint cup (also earthenware) filled up with cider. And of course we would deal the cards round. Have a drink. Play your cards and have a drink. Then we would get down so far on this gallon jug and he'd get the gin bottle out and tip the whole gin bottle in the jug.

The attitude to drinking and driving whether it was a car, a horse and cart, a lorry or a bus was very different from nowadays:

In those days there was no worry about drinking and driving. Coming back across the moors, they say about seeing two white lines, and I've seen two white lines. Which one do I drive to? And you'd slow right down and then on the moor on a long straight piece of the road you'd see some lights coming towards you and they must be in the same state as we are. And it seemed weeks before you get close... but we're both going so steady to make sure we don't hit one another. We always got home safe.

There was not a lot of danger of being stopped by the police. It was quite accepted that many men would drink a lot of cider. One lady said:

My grandfather made all his own cider and that's what pickled him in the end.

Countryside activities

Outside the house families enjoyed evening and Sunday afternoon walks together. The fields and hedgerows also provided a good deal of informal activity involving dogs and shotguns, or nets and ferrets, or perhaps a fishing line. Pete Saunders who worked at Whitehall Farm happily remembered those days:

We used to go out with ferrets and net rabbits. Nelson (Read) had a beautiful ferret. She were a good 'un. She suffocated in the end. We pulled out five dead rabbits and she were behind them suffocated. And we used to shoot. Nelson were a good shot and the old man were too. There always used to be partridges about in those days. Nelson could tickle a trout too.

This was pleasure and relaxation with perhaps the added attraction of a game bird or a rabbit to take home. Other people organised shooting parties for friends and neighbours.

A lot of people if they did have their own place they did go round shooting. Dick Brew had a shoot (pheasants) and then when the lake was being filled he used to have duck shoots. He did come out at Lower Gurney and there weren't very many duck there then, but they did have a shoot.

A woman recalled as a child going off with her father:

On Saturday afternoons Father used to go shooting and sometimes I used to go with him and carry the shot and we used to walk right up to Rackledown right up on the top. They used to buy the shoot, him and his brother. Yes, we used to get pheasants, and I can remember snipe, them with the long beak and them that didn't fly straight, woodcock.

There was always interest when the Mendip Farmers Hunt met, as they did until the lake years, at any of the valley villages. Foxes were real pests, even though most people liked to catch sight of them and thought them handsome enough.

We all felt that the hunt did a good job. The foxes needed to be controlled. Everyone would go and watch them move off. I went hunting whenever I could and on a good day it was thrilling. I had to stop when I was pregnant but in a few years my daughter was in the Pony Club so it didn't end there. The vets, Chivers and Gardner, both hunted and some of the better off farmers. It wasn't just how well you could afford it. It was how keen you were.

Once a year there were the Point-to-Point races at Chewton Mendip and that was a favourite day out. Even if it was the only race meeting they attended, a lot of local people went there for an exciting day.

Outside the farm

The leisure activities and entertainment of the community was a rather individual matter. It is not possible to regard all people as alike. There were men who spent time in the local public houses on a regular basis. For some, adjourning to the Prince of Waterloo when they had concluded their business at Winford Market was a part of their enjoyment. On the other hand there were families who never let a drop of alcohol pass their lips. During the 19th and early 20th century there were many more small drinking houses to serve the miners and agricultural workers but by the 1930s the number of village pubs was much as we know today. In public houses apart from gossip and sometimes singing, the favourite entertainment was to play games such as darts, table skittles and the popular shove ha'penny. This was a local favourite and a most skilful game. The pubs in the valley formed leagues and played in tournaments for a trophy and the competition was taken quite seriously.

Skittles was based in pubs and it wasn't darts early on, it was rings. Similar to a dartboard but it had hooks on it and you had to throw rings on. I can remember darts coming in. Both shops (in Bishop Sutton) had a ring board as well. You would go in and about eight or ten lads used to gather up in there and play rings against each other.

Other games that had their programme of match fixtures were football and cricket and all the villages had their teams. Tennis was also played but less widely. Bishop Sutton in particular was well represented for sport:

Blue Bowl Darts Team: (back row) Arthur Chappell, Sam Wyatt, John Chapman, Jim Saunders, Ted Baker, Bert Hearse, Tom Field, Harry Hudson, Bill Seward, Jack Blacker (landlord), (front row) Annie Dando, Vic Taviner, Mrs Saunders, Mrs Blacker.

They ran four (football) *teams in Bishop Sutton at one time. I think all the villages had teams at one time. Football was the winter months and then most people switched to cricket or tennis. But I never played cricket. The ball was too hard! I played tennis. There were no leagues* (for tennis) *in those days; it was all friendlies between villages, more social than competitive. You played to win but nothing too serious. Some were serious. We had one or two players who got as far as the Redland Championship; that was the big one for this area. Leonard Lovell was pretty good and my cousin Lily Treasurer.*

On the other side of the valley a man clearly recalled playing cricket for Chew Stoke:

We used to have an annual match with the Bournemouth Electricity Company in Bournemouth. We would take a coach down and that was a day out for the Cricket Club. They would take their wives and their sweethearts. The ladies would go into Bournemouth and we would play cricket. There would be a few pints in the club at lunchtime and then we would stop on the way back and have a few more. They used to do a return trip but they were much too good for us. By golly, they got us all out for twelve once!

There were all kinds of other village competitions too with annual fetes and flower show classes being strongly contested.

Chew Magna was the main one for flower shows where we (children) *used to show our writing and painting and that from school. It was held on the topside of the Convent entrance. It was a big field. Then there was Clutton Flower Show.*

Over in Bishop Sutton:

The British Legion always ran a big fair with roundabouts, swings and dodgems and a gymkhana. The gymkhana was where the football pitches are now, behind the village hall and I remember them having the fair across the road and along a bit. Hillside Gardens are there now. A Flower Show as well in a marquee with vegetables and produce. My Dad used to win all the prizes for his beans. And there was a dance in the evening. Oh, that was a big day.

Chew Stoke Harvest Home

Chew Stoke Harvest Home was a great day in the valley too and was awaited with impatience by old and young alike. This used to be an old-fashioned country celebration and friends and relatives from all over the valley met up there. Some of them might not see each other from one year's end to the next otherwise.

We thoroughly enjoyed it. That's where a lot of the locals met their partners at the Harvest Supper.

In the thirties it was held down in the field behind the garage. It's all houses now. Then it moved to the top cross opposite what was Radfords, where they play cricket now. We had a marquee. 'Course everybody had a garden in those days and grew vegetables and the ladies used to exhibit knitted and sewn garments, flowers, eggs, wine and cider – all the country fare – and win prizes for it. The children showed wild flowers and handwriting, painting and catching the most cabbage white butterflies which were great pests!

In fairness the Harvest Home still continues even today but in the old days when every farm worker had his plot the best of them were intense in their rivalry for the quality of their vegetables and flowers. All classes were closely contested. There were also competitions for the best cow kale and cow cabbage and the best hay sample and the best mangel worzel.

Chew Stoke Harvest Home Committee: (back row) J Somers, G West, E Keel, S Morgan, R Warr, Geo Martin, J Bennett, J Say, Wm Gibson, T Payne, J Russell, J Weaver, H Cox. (front row) Jim King ,Wm King, M J Croker.

I was on the committee for a while. I suppose at about eight in the morning we would erect the display tables with white sheets of paper and people would start bringing in their produce; turnips, swedes, mangels, flowers and all the other exhibits. I think they cleared the tent about twelve o'clock for the judges to come in. And then at one o'clock all the committee and the judges sat down to a salad lunch with a pint of beer in the marquee. The judges would say a few words and the show would open at two o'clock, a wonderful day.

There was also skittling for a pig, and a band, and foot races, and a grand Tug of War tournament. This last was taken very seriously and the teams of miners and quarrymen from other areas of the Mendips trained hard for it. After that the beer tent was very popular with these gentlemen. The tea tent was popular with the ladies. At one time the tables were allotted to the ladies of the committee and they each brought their own cloth and china and decorated it with an arrangement of flowers. There was a prize for the prettiest. The evening concluded with a dance in the marquee to a nice band. Meanwhile the young ones were in their element on the 'Golden Gallopers' roundabout and the swing boats and other rides at the funfair provided by Coles. (They were all powered by Masterpiece a steam engine now in preservation at Alan Sparkes). They looked forward to it all summer. We have talked to several elderly ladies who said that all the pocket money they earned in the summer by selling primroses and picking fruit and so on was saved up for them by their parents and given to them to spend at the Harvest Home.

Churches

The churches within the valley had far wider support than nowadays. There were Church of England ministries within all villages and either Baptist or Methodist chapels in most but there was only one Catholic chapel, St Michaels, East Harptree. However, whatever the denomination, they were all well attended. It was very much a matter of individual family conscience. Some families attended three or four times on a Sunday while others only sent the children to Sunday school. For many their village church was also the centre of all their social activities as all the churches and chapels in the valley also organised socials, little fetes, whist drives and beetle drives. 'There were film shows at the Church hall on Saturdays.' Then there was the church Ladies Circle, and the choirs. They could be a very long-term commitment. Arthur Wilson farmer and miller at Stratford Mill was organist at West Harptree:

Dad used to take a very active part in the village. He wasn't home a lot. 33 years he did in all at the church and he was choirmaster as well there, you see. And he taught organ as well.

A gentleman who attended church at Chew Stoke recalled:

We had a choir of about ten boys and eight men and you had two services every Sunday and a lot of people at church. During the thirties we had several choirmasters. The one I remember had to cycle out from Bristol and we used to take it in turns to give him lunch. But we had a couple more and the one that remained was called Mr Thistlewaite. He was a wonderful choirmaster.

We used to sing anthems associated with all the different Christian festivals like Christmas, Advent, Easter, Whitsun, Trinity and Harvest. We used to go to the annual festival of music at Wells Cathedral. I think that was held in high summer. And you would get as many as 1000 voices from different choirs singing. It was a wonderful experience. I was in the choir for 65 years. I went from the boys' into the men's. Now we've got no choir at all.

Bell ringers were a little different. In many villages they never went to the services; they just rang the bells!

In the thirties we had six bells and we had a very good band of ringers. They didn't go to church, they just liked to ring the bells. The bells would be rung properly every Sunday morning and father would operate the chimes in the evening. You had a pulley mechanism so that one man can ring all the bells and play tunes. We had no bell ringers after the War so five or six choir men decided to have a go and brought in one or two more. We had no lady ringers until after the War.

The churches, as a reward to the choristers and Sunday school children for their regular attendance, also arranged annual outings. Latterly these took the form of a coach trip to the seaside, Weston-Super-Mare being the favoured venue. As it was a rare treat to go there in the days when cars were scarce and not available to the ordinary villager, this was an exciting event.

National movements

In the twenties and thirties there were local branches of national movements in the valley as elsewhere. There was the British Legion, which was active in Bishop Sutton and Chew Stoke, and the National Farmers Union, while the Young Farmers Club was of great importance to the young generation. For the ladies the Women's Institute was a social outlet and a source of ideas. The meetings drew together many whose horizons might otherwise have been narrow. It gave them a voice and a sense of their own worth as members of a community. It is easy enough to smile at the apparent concentration on domestic skills but they were, after all, the practical realities of women's lives and there was a lot more to the movement than that. Many of the speakers brought new insights and the resolutions to be presented to the national conference were of more than parochial interest. At the same time the reality of a social hierarchy in the countryside has to be acknowledged. To quote one of our informants, 'I was never a member of the WI. I think it was looked on as a classy sort of thing.' Certainly a basic level of education and ability was required to organise events and manage a meeting, but the experience was valuable and empowering to many.

There was respect shown to the professional classes. One woman told us that 'even now I cannot be any different, in speaking to a doctor or an old teacher, even when invited to use first names.' When customers came to settle their accounts at local shops and businesses they were always called Mr or Mrs. Another man said to us:

If the doctor asked for something, it would happen. The hierarchy in those days was still quite marked. Lord Strachey was at the top.

The same thing applied to the National Farmers Union. It was the more prosperous and established farmer who tended to be represented, and to be a leader in the movement implied both business and practical resources. The NFU had a political voice and in those days at least it was listened to. The social side featured annual dinners and dances where the ladies were present. Practical skills were encouraged by competitions in ploughing, hedging and ditching, thatching and so on. The annual ploughing matches were a popular day out and the beautiful work that was on show was much admired. There were classes at all levels and some went as far as to compete at national level.

The Young Farmers Club was a strong influence on the farming community and very popular. Chew Valley Young Farmers was formed in 1931 and a number of those that we talked to were early members. It had the support and backing of the Ministry of Agriculture and the approval of most parents and above all it was thoroughly enjoyed by the young people. Its purposes were primarily educational and it worked to inform and train its members in husbandry and stockmanship, but more than that it had a social value that cannot be overestimated. It is always said that it acted like a marriage bureau for it brought together a crowd of young people of similar backgrounds who might otherwise have remained socially isolated. So many of the farming families we have talked to originated from contacts made at Young Farmers meetings or rallies.

There were lectures and instruction in a wide range of subjects and competitions in stock judging and calf rearing and ploughing and hedging. For the girls there was also poultry dressing and cake making. Nowadays of course the male/female division is less marked! To be selected to compete in a major show must have been a thrill and the trip a real adventure, even if it did entail riding a bicycle into Temple Meads to take a train to London as one boy did! During the war they struggled to get to the meetings through the blackout and were encouraged to invite the land girls along. In some years meetings had to be curtailed due to Foot and Mouth outbreaks, but it is still going strong. The third generation of members is now represented in some families. Jane King made a summary of the club from 1931 until 2001 from records and minute books. The range of talks and activities was tremendous.

John Curry, who grew up at Moreton Farm, was one of the founder members along with John King,

> *I went to the Young Farmers in Chew Magna. John King and me and there were two Russells from Winford, they were twins, Nelson Read and Fred Cole. I learnt quite a bit there. It was like it is today, a matrimonial business.*

Another farmer said:

> *They did stock judging. I was more interested in the pedigree breeding of*

animals. They organised all sorts of social activities.

Nelson Read always maintained that the best education he ever had was at Young Farmers. But the dances were important functions too and they are still remembered:

I went to the Young Farmers at Chew Magna. We would go to the different Young Farmers dances 'cause they would have them in most village halls. Big ones would be down at Wells.

Dances

It cannot simply be the lively and interesting personalities of those who are still around to talk with us that accounts for the importance of the dance in their recollections. We are not short of accounts of dancing. It must have played a large part in the social life of the villages. It may seem strange now, but most of these local dances were held without a bar. It isn't very surprising however that the male half of the company failed to arrive until after the pub closed.

We had dances in the church hall (Chew Stoke). Looking back we always had what we called 'A Grand Dance'. Then we realised that wasn't very appropriate so we called it afterwards 'Come Dancing'. The funny thing was, they only had curtains half-way up the windows, so when I was a lad we used to climb up the trees outside in the dark so we could look down and see it all lit up inside and see what was happening. Up to ten o'clock all you could see was girls all round the room, new hairstyle, lovely dance dress and patent shoes you know, but there weren't any men. When the Yew Tree turned out at ten o'clock they all come flooding in and they all jumped on their feet and away they went. There was no bar at these dances. They would have to go to the Yew Tree to get tanked up, you see, to give them enough courage to ask a girl on the floor.

And then we had the dances. I suppose I was about fourteen when I first went. There weren't many boys around because they were mostly in the army so we always used to have to dance with each other but we had a good time. We didn't have dancing lessons as such we just picked it up watching other ones. The Dashing White Sergeant, the Military Two Step, Waltzes and the Foxtrots obviously and Quickstep.

I went to lessons at the village hall (Bishop Sutton). Used to be a chappie, Albert Bigwell, used to come from Radstock way. He and his wife were good dancers and they used to run an evening class. Mostly young people paid sixpence to go and learn to dance.

I used to love dancing. Years ago the dances we had were so much better than today. We used to go to the Hunt Balls, National Farmers Union dances and the Police Balls. That's where I met my wife at a Police Ball. The Hunt balls were always held at Wells Town Hall or Wells Mental Hospital (they had a lovely hall), and Downside. We used to go to one or two every week. Every Saturday, but it could be Wednesday night, anytime really. Usually eight o'clock to twelve was the normal dance. Don Harris at Hinton Blewett he was a great friend of mine and he had this band and he would always inform us where he was playing and we used to go. Occasionally we would go by bike but generally we could scrape up a car.

My Dad used to MC all the village dances. He was just like a fairy on his feet. He used to put his tails on and his dickey bow. I used to go from when I was twelve or thirteen and Dad used to bring me home. We all went and we all joined in. I went right up until I got married. We used to go to Chewton Mendip, Farrington Gurney, Chew Stoke, anywhere. Maurice Symes Band, oh, he was good. We had some really lovely times. Sometimes we would go in Dad's car and sometimes we would ride with friends. We would do the old Lancers, the Moonlight Saunter, the Waltz Cotillion – that's an old fashioned one. Tea and bickies, not the booze then. They'd have their helpers and they'd take them round on little trays and of course we would wear our long frocks. We used to dress up to go to our local dances.

By 1936 I was playing with the West Harptree Band called the Live Wires. That was a five piece: saxophone, that was Ron Veater the butcher; Percy Bath played the piano accordion; Sandy Powell on piano; myself on drums. They played all around the valley, Chew Magna, Chew Stoke, West Harptree, Bishop Sutton and Compton Martin.

Then I played the double bass with the Don Harris Dance Band. Don, from Hinton Blewett but originally from Sutton, had a big ten piece band but normally it was a five or six piece for these local dances. There were regular dances. There was usually one every week but we played every two or three weeks.

It was near enough the same people every week, we just went from one village to another. We danced Valettas, Barn Dance, Quick Step, Waltz, Palais Glide, Hokey Cokey, and Foxtrot...We never really got into Rock 'n Roll. We always had to put a bit of Old Time in because there was all age groups. It was not all young people.

Most of those dances were a shilling to go in. We would play from eight to twelve for ten shilling each. We've played eight to two and we'd get paid a pound each then. Then occasionally you would get a posh one, evening dress, long down to the ground, and that would be two and six pence to go in. That would be like the tennis club, or the cricket club, or the British Legion. And the Church ran posh dances. It was still in the village hall and they'd trim the hall up for those functions. Ladies would wear long dresses and the men evening dress. They used to get a ten-piece band up from Weston-Super-Mare once a year. That was a big affair. That would be rather posh.

We always stopped for refreshments, at the big ones anyway, sandwiches or something. I don't think there was anything at the hops. Running a dance was the only way to raise funds really, or a whist drive and later on Bingo.

Progress however, cannot be stopped and even in the valley Rock 'n Roll caught on in the end.

I played into the sixties until I gave up. I remember Don saying to me one day, 'There's a new rhythm out – a new beat'.

I said, 'You can only have waltz time or quickstep time, either beating four to the bar or three to the bar. What else can you have?'

'Oh, this is in between. It's going to be bad for us.'

And of course this was disco music and within two or three years bands were out more or less.

Amateur dramatics and concerts

There were also concerts and pantomimes and plays put on by local drama societies and often a film show. There was no end to the activities available. Let no one imagine that country life was dull and quiet, it was anything but! Of course how much any particular family participated was a matter of choice.

And then we had the Rev. Cresswell Hicks and Steven his son and he used to put on all these pantomimes called the Arcadians. We were all in that, my sisters and I. He used to get up some lovely things, you know. We used to do a pantomime most years and I used to do leading boy in that. The Vicar used to write that and it was very popular. I can remember going to Winford and Chewton Mendip and I think we went to Compton one year.

I came to Chew Magna in 1949 at the same time as Ken Roberts who was the Chief Engineer for the Lake with Bristol Water. We both quite quickly became involved with Chew Magna Players, the local dramatic group and that was a lot of fun. Dr Hughes was the moving force in it. We used to tour; one of our venues was the theatre at East Harptree. As doctor in the village he could get things moving.

The Harptree Arcadians: (back row) Mrs Seward, Miss Stevens, Donald Melton, Mr Bawden, Mrs Wyatt, Sid Edwards, Laura Paddock, Maurice Symes, Miss Weaver, Mrs Sam Wyatt, Anita Blannin, Nelly Gaywood, Edna Blannin, Ginny Farrow. (row 2) Mrs Keedwell, Gwen Noakes, Lou Baber, Audrey Wilson, Pat Seward, Bill Seward, Ethel Dix, Doreen Body, Norah Moon, Jim Wyatt, Bob Dury. (row 3) Pam Warford, Sybil Moulder, Brenda Wilson, Lorna Paines, Joan Barton, Ruth Daniels, Ena Body. (row 4) Rod Moon, Cyril Downer, Mrs Diamond, Rev. Cresswell Hicks, Mrs Hicks, Olive Symes, Pop Gaywood, Ron Harvey, Tom Wyatt. (front row) Ronnie Wyatt, Janet Wilson, Mollie Paines, Mr Braine, Bill King, Dawn Bristow, Colin Symes, John Steven Hicks, David Blannin, Harold Taviner, David Bawden.

There were also more professional travelling shows.

> *You used to get touring concerts who came to the village hall for a week. Freddie Fay and his Frolics, wasn't it? Freddie was a comedian and there was a girl who did acrobatics. It was a family thing and I should think there were about seven or eight of them. They used to come and stay in the village. The old Sutton Village hall was one of the bigger village halls. It was a fair size with a proper stage and dressing rooms and a bar in the corner.*

Courting and marriage

It is plain that all these social activities and associations widened the number of opportunities available to young people in the crucial business of finding a mate.

As we have already more than hinted it was one of the main attractions of the Young Farmers and the local hop was another favourite place to see and be seen. There were of course others:

> *I met my husband at church. He was working for the Forestry Commission up on the Mendips and he used to come down to church and we were introduced. We used to go to classical music concerts at the Central Hall, the Colston Hall. He had a motor bike and we used to go to Cheddar sometimes and Burrington Combe, picnicking and that.*
>
> *I was married at West Harptree Church and then we went to the village hall. Mum and Fanny did the catering.*

Weddings were simpler occasions then and guests were not presented with an expensive present list either!

Another lady interviewed by us met her husband at Chew Stoke Harvest Home when she was sixteen. He joined up a couple of days before conscription because he wanted to get into the Royal Engineers and she wrote to him for seven years as he was abroad most of the time. That was no doubt a typical wartime scenario but is a fine example of fidelity.

In the old days few people married far afield. Choice may have been restricted to a relatively small area but it helped that there was so often a common background and the families knew a good deal about each others' reputation. In those days marriages tended to last a lifetime.

Visitors to the valley

The Chew Valley because of its proximity to Bristol has always attracted city dwellers to its quiet leafy lanes and the tranquillity of the river. On Sundays and public holidays walking and cycling in the countryside were popular escapes from the noise and grime of weekday life.

Not all visitors to the valley returned to Bristol after their day out. Several farms took in paying guests.

> *Denny House Farm was always popular. People used to come for holidays, not B & B then, they would stay for a week full board.*

Locals had always 'fished' in the river but strictly speaking this was poaching. The right to fish in the Chew had belonged to individuals for many years. Originally, these would probably all have belonged to the lords of the manors; for example, in 1630 the lord of the manor of East Harptree had 'a fishing in the river, extending from Sherborne to the church bridge in East Harptree'. By the 1930s however, the fishing rights to most stretches of the river and its tributaries were rented by clubs. Of these the Knowle Angling Association's rights included most of the stretch of the Chew now under the lake. Other clubs included the Golden Carp, the City of Bristol, and Avon and Tributaries. The fishing was mainly for coarse fish and some trout.

As I remember it the Club stocked the water. If you don't stock, you don't have enough fish and the club wouldn't survive. They used to buy the fish.

In the Chew there would be every known fish. Almost any species of fresh water fish existed in some part. You wouldn't get big fish in the shallower parts but when you got down to... there would be everything. You don't expect to find any water that hasn't got pike in it and they are a menace because they love fish. I can remember the dace. Now dace will go for your fly but if you think trout fishing with a fly is difficult then try catching dace. You could drop the fly on the water; the dace will come, take hold of it and spit it out before you can blink. I reckon you might catch one for every 100 fish. There were chub in the river. I can remember that because chub is quite a nice fish and on the Knowle water you could catch one a pound and a half.

Fishing is still such an important part of the landscape of the Chew Lake. Let us finish this chapter therefore, with the following account which gives some idea of how different it used to be fishing on the River Chew:

In those days if I were going fishing it meant cycling all the way from Bristol (Ashton Gate). My half-day was Wednesday and if I didn't catch a fish Wednesday afternoon then Thursday lunch was egg and chips!

The chap I went fishing with was the best fisherman I ever knew and taught me all I know about fishing. He was a bait fisherman as we say; he drowned worms and things like that. He liked to go to Moreton Mill because he would put a tiny little hook on with a bit of bread or something and below it was a No. 8, a bigger hook. He'd drop it in this mill-race, where the water falls, then the little fish, the little minnows, would take this tiny little bit of bread on a very small hook. Then he'd take that minnow off the small hook, put it on the big hook and drop it back in the pool again. We came home with a bag full of trout. But I became interested in fly-fishing and you couldn't fly-fish there because the bank was virtually covered over with vegetation. So I used to go on up towards Stratford (Mill) and that was all open bank.

You would often catch a trout that weighed say a pound and a quarter. The further upstream you went, the stream got narrower and shallower. It was much more difficult to catch the trout.

I used to get upset if I saw another angler.

Part of the joy of fishing was the environment. One great thing in those days – we had otters and we used to curse them. I was sat on the river bank one day, minding my own business, fishing quietly in this cow drink as we called it (where the cows went in to drink – a good place to fish because the cows stirred up the mud and therefore food for the fish) and I heard this curious barking noise. I turned round – an otter. That otter wanted to go in the cow drink and he was letting me know. Eventually the penny dropped and I moved away and that blasted otter went in there and within two minutes he was out with a trout, walking back up the bank.

I've also fallen asleep and lost food to water creatures, water voles. Some of them were quite big. Stoats were very prevalent in those days and if you wanted to see kingfishers, go to the Chew but we didn't have cormorants in those days, thank God.

CHAPTER ELEVEN

The War Years

War affected everyone's lives although for many in the countryside the routine of everyday life continued much as usual but with various inconveniences that could hardly be ignored. The prohibition on showing any kind of light at night for instance must have made a difference when tending lambing ewes or even moving churns of milk around after dark. 'The blackout was very important. A warden went round checking.' In the villages there were Air Raid Wardens but it is doubtful if outlying farmsteads saw too much of them.

> *To drive at night we had to have proper masks on the headlamps. The lights weren't very bright then but by the time you put masks on them, like slots, you could hardly see. We managed but you didn't reckon to go out too much at night. It had to be an emergency or something like that.*

Petrol supplies were strictly controlled.

> *Petrol rationing came in and everybody had coupons. Petrol that was used for agriculture or say by doctors or somebody like that, well they were allowed a bit more because of travelling round. It was a bit tight for some.*

Agricultural fuel contained a red dye (as it still does, but now due to the lower tax paid) and it could be 'dipped' by inspectors to check that the vehicle was not using red petrol on a social occasion. There were various ways of getting around this. One farmer's son carried a pig around with him in the back of his truck when he was visiting his young lady.

Fear of bombing

Even in the country, relatively safe though it was, there was a fear of enemy action as there was a perception that as soon as war was declared the Germans were fully prepared to invade. As one man said:

> *I was by the garage getting a can of paraffin when it came over the radio that war was declared and I said to th' horse, 'C'mon John. Let's get on home before they bombers start comin' over'.*

When the blitz really did start in earnest, although the countryside was not the real target there was plenty of evidence as to what was happening. There were many incidences of stray bombs and shrapnel from anti-aircraft shells which killed the odd cow!

> *It was a nerve-racking time. You felt safer* (in the country) *obviously 'cause you could see it all around you anyway. You could watch the bombing of Bristol; you could hear the bombs go down and see the flames go up. And you could see Bath and Weston, the sirens going and incendiaries.*

> *We had several bombs out round here dropped. That's when they just let them go so they could get back home. I believe at Compton Martin there was a family killed there. Don Harris, up in Hinton Blewett, he was sat in his hut by Prospect Stile, he had a lovely view of the valley there, a bomb come down, and a piece of shrapnel went right through the shed and into his shoulder.*

> *We had quite a few bombs dropped around Stowey and Sutton. We had a lot of incendiary bombs. They were quite frightening.*

A rain of incendiary bombs could be a menace in a farmyard and it was up to the family who lived there to extinguish them as fast as they could before the buildings caught fire. It was no use waiting for the fire brigade. Most people hid under a table during air raids but some had shelters.

> *We had an air raid shelter in the garden when the War was on. Anderson shelters were not available in the country areas. They were supplied in the towns because they were more vulnerable anyway. People made their own. What most people did was find somewhere where there was a bank and tunnel in. We made one down here but I don't think we ever went in it. It was there if you needed it. If you had a cellar you could use that.*

> *We took our mattresses over to Henry Strachey's cellar. A couple of times a week, all through the War we would go, taking our own bedding.*

> *When they were bombing in Bristol you could almost read the newspaper in our*

back porch. It was all lit up. I remember once going out on my bike and this German plane came over and we heard the bullets hitting an old galvanised shed. And then we had the ack-ack guns and the searchlights. That was quite handy actually. It was a comfort sometimes.

And of course they lit fires as well to attract them (the planes). *There was a decoy near Chew Magna.*

On the top of the Pit at Bishop Sutton there was an ack-ack gun, big powerful guns, and of course when that opened up... They (Germans) *chucked bombs down at the top of the road. The idea was to keep them out of Bristol and get them to unload them out here. The Army, I suppose eight or ten of them, who manned the gun, were based in houses around the village. A lot were down at Chew Park Farm.*

At the top of Stowey Hill there was a search light. There were a lot of soldiers at Stowey. They had their own living accommodation there – a hut. The girls would all walk up from Sutton...

When we used to go to Temple Cloud (dances) *the soldiers were all there dancing.*

There were servicemen and women in a number of places around the valley manning anti-aircraft sites, and towards D Day, invasion forces were concentrating on the Mendips.

War service

During the War there were changes in the population. Some men and women went off to the armed services. Some went willingly; it opened up opportunities which they might never have had otherwise in a rural area.

Going into the Army was a godsend for me. It got me out of gardening. It broke everything up. I don't think I would have made a gardener.

Others were less willing. In WW1 there were farmers who were anxious to protect their sons from military service. Oscar Walker is recorded as saying:

My Father were on the tribunal and of course he tried to get farm labourers off because, you know, it was essential to try to keep them. And of course every bloody farmer in they days, he wanted to keep his sons out of the War, and they all wanted to see him, offering him money and all that, but of course he didn't take it.

Their successors in WW2 were understandably almost as anxious to find a more congenial role also. Many were in reserved occupations, 'key men in agriculture' and so on. Most of them had some sort of civil defence duties or were swept up into the Home Guard. Girls too had to register and could be called up. One woman whose father worked as gardener to Lord Strachey remembered that her father didn't want her to be called up for the Land Army so he spoke to Lord Stratchey and she was employed as a horticultural worker under her father:

I was then in a reserved occupation. Lord Strachey did a kindness for us really.

Many women had to take in evacuees and a lot worked in the munitions factories. Bath had the biggest one and they would bus people in. And there was something at Hallatrow. Women (until) *then weren't working in that kind of work. They were just told that was what they had to do and they had to do it. And of course they were also called up for the forces, Army, Navy, Air Force and those that didn't were put into factories to work for the war effort.*

At the outbreak of war I volunteered for the Army because all my friends were gone in the army and I felt I wanted to go, and so I went to Chew Magna to register at the Labour Exchange. I knew the man personally. That was Walt Spear. And I said that I wanted to register as a general labourer. And he said, 'Oh, you'll be in the Forces in six weeks. You know that, do you?'

And I said, 'Well, that's the general idea'. I didn't particularly want to volunteer but I didn't mind being called up. I was about seventeen and half or eighteen then.

Then within about two or three weeks my dad died so I went back and re-registered then, 'cause otherwise if I had gone my mum would have been left with the farm. So then I was in a reserved occupation.

There were a few young lads also working on the farms. And of course in the pits all the miners were in a reserved occupation.

So I volunteered for the next best thing, the Home Guard. It was either that or ARP or the Auxiliary Fire Service. I think if you volunteered you could join whichever one you wanted. But my dad was in the Army, a soldier from the First World War, and I suppose I felt I would like to be a soldier as well.

Everyone had some part to play. This was 'total war', even in so quiet a place. The Safety Officer at Bromley Pit was in charge of a First Aid Post for instance. Some, like Mr Young and Mr Sparkes were in the Special Constabulary. A former policeman told us:

During the War the police were on the alert and they had lots of Special Constables. They would be given police duties to do where they were stretched. They were mature men. We had three or four here. They had a uniform, a flat cap, and they were never paid.

When Bristol was being bombed you would get people who had cars tearing out from Bristol to get away from the blitz, and we were positioned with cars at different spots to stop them from coming out. You wanted them back in town fighting the fires; they were able-bodied men. One position I was in was at the crossroads at Churchill.

Even children did their bit:

During the War I belonged to the Women's Junior Air Corp. at Compton Martin. What good we would have done if the invasion came, I don't know. We used to march up and down and do first aid. I was born in 1923 so I was only sixteen. We didn't go out observing or anything like that.

Children also helped collect anything that could be of value recycled for the war effort, newspaper, scrap metal, glass.

Evacuees

There was another responsibility that countrywomen took on during the War and most of them bore it cheerfully and with generosity. As if there was not enough to do caring for her own children anyone with a spare room would find themselves with evacuees billeted on them. There were some evacuees who felt so out of their element in the country that they stayed for only a very short time. Some of these were women with small babies from the East End of London and their ways were not those of the local people. They were seen sitting on the steps of the Stoke Inn feeding their babies and giving the small children bread torn from a loaf. This came as a culture shock to the village! On the other hand there were families who showed their devotion in very touching ways. Margaret Holmes tells how the husband of one woman used to cycle down from London at weekends to see his family. Some people who had evacuees also became very attached to them and are still in touch. This was evident from comments made by those who were local people at the time:

I can only speak for my own mother-in-law here. She was a natural mother and the children who were with her were treated as members of the family and were very happy. The surviving one is still in contact with us and remembers farm life in the Chew Valley as an experience that shaped her future.

We had evacuees during the War. They mostly came from London. I just had the children on their own. I had a letter from the Queen Mother thanking me for my service. I was the only one in East Harptree got one.

Mother brought up six children and during the war we had three evacuees, two from London and one from Bristol.

We had the evacuees. They were families with ten and twelve-year-old kids. Mum had about two or three lots. There was quite a bit to do with the cooking

The orchard at Stratford Mill with Arthur Wilson and two visitors. (Valerie Dean, who was holidaying in the BWW cottage at the Mill, with Jacqueline Cheek.)

as well. She did work hard. I was maybe about four or five and I remember them panicking one night. They were Bristol people and we had heard this terrible bang. Mum thought maybe a bomb had been dropped over Bath way. They all got under the table anyway, screeching and screaming.

People came out of Bristol for short breaks to escape the bombings.

Part of Stratford Mill farmhouse was a separate cottage. During the War it was made available to Bristol Waterworks' staff to take a break away from the bombing. My Father was an accountant with the Company and I spent several holidays there with my parents. I was approximately thirteen at the time. Our luggage was sent out by Bristol Waterworks and so we didn't have to worry about that. We cycled out from our home in Stoke Bishop and spent time exploring the Mendip area, walking and cycling. I think we stayed for a week in the summer but it might have been a fortnight.

I went to visit a friend from school in Bristol who was staying in a house on the main Blue Bowl to Chew Stoke road. I think her family were there to get away from the bombing too.

It was such a lovely old farm and such an idyllic situation with the pond and the river. During the War they used to have lots of scouts and messenger boys come out from Bristol to camp. They used to have big camps. We used to have marvellous times actually. We all went swimming. I went on a tandem with one of the lads to his home for a week. So it really opened up quite a few opportunities.

Rationing

Food rationing applied to everyone but the advantages of being a country dweller are not to be underestimated. Townspeople had no real means of supplementing the rations they were strictly entitled to, whereas farmers and their friends and neighbours had much more freedom. In the first place they had first call on eggs and dairy produce. No one could prevent them from taking enough cream from the milk churns to make their own butter, or for that matter a bit of cheese. Poultry and game were always available and killing a pig, lamb or calf could be arranged when required. The only advantage urban dwellers had was the privilege of queuing for hours to buy a piece of cod, or even a whale meat steak! It was not unknown for teenagers from town to be sent on a twelve-mile bicycle ride into the country to visit a friendly farmer who had promised to sell them half a dozen eggs. Of course it wasn't strictly according to the rules but that was the way of it.

During the War you were allocated a certain amount of (feed) *depending how many poultry or pigs you had. There was generally enough food. I think animals were looked after probably better than the human beings, although nobody starved and I think people were fitter.*

Anyone with pigs was allowed one pig to keep in exchange for their bacon ration entitlement and was supposed to send any further ones to the ministry, but this regulation was better honoured in the breach than the observance. Various ruses were employed to conceal the butchery from the neighbours and above all from the local policeman!

You could get permission to kill a pig, on licence, for your own use. You usually shared it with your next door neighbour, they paid you for half of it. If you could do it on your own place you had to get permission. Only a few people did it (the killing). *The man I used to get to do it came and killed this pig. We didn't get a licence. He said, 'We don't want a licence, we'll soon deal with that'. Anyway he came down, backed his lorry down there and got this pig in. And of course he'd bang him on the head with the spike, cut his throat and then bleed him. But that pig would not go down. I shall never forget that. Squeal? Oh dear. And we were nearly all in white shirts and we were splattered with blood. The pig was squealing. I was frightened. I could swear they could hear him along Chew Stoke where the copper lived. Anyway eventually he bled him, lit a fire down here, burnt the bristle off and scraped him and dressed it. He did it all and then we shared it. And this was all against the law.*

It was bacon and we put it in brine in a bath up in the bedroom behind the wardrobe. And one day I noticed a patch in the corner of the dining room ceiling. The bath had started to leak. Brine, it's funny stuff, it must have eaten the solder!

When the War came, 1939, Dad was given one slaughterhouse to work from. So he had to make money any way he could. In Bristol everybody had two bins, one for food scraps, the swill. It would be collected, taken to a plant in Eastville and cooked into what they called Tottenham Pudding; it was like a cake. He would go to Eastville at 3am in the morning, collect as many Tottenham Puddings as they would allow him and sell them. The farmers would take a few, but people like Mrs Farrow, at Rock House would have a half. Most people would have a pig in their garden and with a bit of meal mixed with the pudding they could feed it quite well.

During the War Mr Todd used to keep rabbits instead of poultry and we used to slaughter them. We had to cut the poultry down 'cause the feed was rationed and we couldn't get the feed. But we could feed rabbits with dandelions and things like that. He had a round in Bristol and he'd sell them on a Thursday with eggs and poultry. 'Cause everybody was looking for something 'cause there was nothing to be had.

There was a lot of changes during the War. We had goats on the farm at Mr Todd's. And we used to milk the goats and my Father used to make cheese with the milk and Mr Todd used to sell that in Bristol 'cause people used to only get a teeny little cheese ration.

We did quite well. We were always getting rabbits and then there might be pheasants. (The pheasants belonged to Dr Brew!)

Another factor that made country people more independent was the tradition of vegetable growing. 'Dig for Victory' was a national slogan but not everyone in town had a good area of garden, whilst farmers and farm labourers had both space and expertise.

The War Agricultural Committee

Although some crops were grown to supply cattle feed, mainly kale and roots, there were few farms that had either suitable land, or indeed the equipment, or even the skills necessary to grow cereals. Yet during WW2 they were required to plough up a certain percentage of it for that purpose. England had to be fed and the convoys of ships running the Atlantic blockade carried other and more urgent cargoes. There was a strict limit to the amount of foodstuffs that could be imported. Home grown barley and wheat and oats were required.

During the War they tried to emphasise to grow corn because they were concerned about the German submarines. There were men even from our village who were serving in the Merchant Navy who were lost on the North Atlantic or Baltic convoys. We owed it to them to do what we could.

Farms at Chew Park, Widcombe and Whitehall, where there was some drier ground, had the advantage and no great difficulty in filling their quota. They could use outlying land and get a decent yield. Less fortunate farmers were nevertheless instructed by the War Agricultural Committee to plough this piece or that and would do their best. In some cases they were not skilled at arable work and lacked the equipment so they had either to buy machinery or employ a contractor to do the work:

During the War we had to plough a percentage of land. The two Agricultural Committee representatives would come around and tour the area and ask you to plough a bit of land. You were told what acreage to do. Nobody wanted to and we didn't have the machinery. You had to go and get it. We got a plough and a tractor and drags and things. I think you could choose your crop more or less.

I did some ploughing for Mr Edward Mapstone at Denny Farm. I don't think they had ploughed before the War.

I would think that all down through there (the valley bottom) *could be a bit on the damp side. There was very little cereals grown down through there during the War years. None of it at Moreton but Denny was a bit higher. I ploughed for Mr Wooley down by the Blue Bowl and all down the lane there and for Mr King at West Harptree, all cereal growing there.*

Even Dr Brew at Chew Magna who had some land up on top Burledge Common got me to go up there to plough this land for him and it was ever so stony and rough. Oh, that was a rough job. But he was pleased he had some buckwheat for his pheasants.

The 'War Ag. Committee' was not popular with many people but it had to be respected as it had real powers:

The Government Agricultural Committee was mostly run by farmers to tell other farmers what to do with their land. That caused some resentment. They didn't like to be told what to do with their own land but at the end of it, they did do it because they were forced to.

Wilfred Middle, he was a farmer on it and Charlie Gay up at Hinton Blewett. At East Harptree, Mr Rendle Drew was on it. I know my Father was asked to but he declined. He said he had enough to do, to do it properly and he knew that he would upset some. A lot of people grumbled about it, if they were told to do something and they didn't want to.

The Committee would all go to Taunton for these meetings and discuss what had to be done. Everything was done from Taunton. And then they would come back and see the farmer and tell him what to do. It was some job. The Agricultural Committee brought quite a lot (rules and regulations) *in but there have been lots since.*

Women's Land Army

While prisoners of war were employed on farms throughout Somerset there were none working, as far as we have been able to ascertain, on any of the farms within the valley. There is a well-known landmark by the road on the way to Wells. The sculpture of Romulus and Remus suckling from a wolf was made by an Italian POW who worked at that farm.

Land girls however were widely employed. The girls were allocated to specific farms by the Agricultural Committee or worked as contracting teams to make hay and to cultivate arable land and harvest crops. It was marvellous how these girls, some of them from urban backgrounds took to tractor work, or indeed to milking, with very little instruction. Several were happy to marry and spend the rest of their lives here.

We used to get the land girls helping with the threshing quite a bit. They were very good. I know we were somewhere one day threshing and there were some mice there and they ran all up the land girl's trousers. There was a main bit of fun going on and the other one had to go with her and get it out. I've seen all sorts of fun.

One lady who came here during the war as a land girl and now lives in Bishop Sutton was brought up in London and Bolton, Lancashire. She told us:

I did enjoy my time in the Land Army and I made some wonderful friends.

In Bolton I worked for Burton the Tailor doing officers' greatcoats. The War gave us the opportunity to travel.

I was seventeen when I volunteered. We only went for a laugh, a couple of other girls and myself. First of all I went to Pilton, near Shepton, for training, learning to milk cows. They did ask me if I had any preference and I said, 'Well, I don't want to go to Kent or anywhere around London. I'd like to go somewhere different'. And this is where they sent me, North Somerset.

I started off in lodgings in Stanton Drew and I worked for Mrs Marshall at Moorledge in Chew Magna. It was a general farm. Then Mrs Marshall's son died and I went to work for a farmer almost next door to Blackmore and Langdon. Before I went to work for him, Dr Brew came to see me and asked me if I would go and work for him. And I said yes. But a lady from the Land Army came and tore me off a strip. 'You will not get your own employment. You will go where you are sent.' So I couldn't go to Dr Brew because this other gentleman was the next one on the list. So I went to him but I wasn't there a terrible long time, no time at all really, and I just walked out on him because he was such a pig of a man. And the Land Army lady came to see me again and she said, 'Well, you did stay there longer than any of the other girls'. Well, then I could go to Dr Brew.

When I went to Dr Brew that was the only time I worked with another girl but I was going there to take her place. She was getting married. I quite enjoyed that and I was there until I got married.

I used to like driving the horses. I suppose I liked the pace of the horses. I disliked poultry – never have liked birds.

Tractors then were very simple. Somebody just showed you the basics and you got on with it. Well you had to, didn't you? It was rather that than the Army and all those places.

Another Land Army girl, this time from London, who married a local man, had received her call up paper at eighteen. She had wanted to go in the Air Force because she liked the colour of the uniform but this was not to be:

You could give your choice but they were full up. I didn't want Army or Navy so ended up in the Land Army.

I enjoyed it. It was something different to London. I was happy to go. It was an adventure. We couldn't choose we were just told where we had to go. I had to go to Clutton and I thought, where the… is that? I had to meet up with three other girls at Paddington Station and we travelled to Frome and then to Clutton.

A car met us with the man who was going to be our boss. He had a shed for an office at our depot which was a farm on the main road at Temple Cloud. We were the first girls. He had men under him as well. There was a lorry to transport us. But they supplied us with a bike if we didn't have one.

I had digs with one of the other girls at Clutton. We shared a room and our meals were provided. They were stopped out of our wages.

I was going to be a tractor driver and working for the Agricultural Committee. The first couple of days I felt terribly sick just with the smell of the calves. It took me a couple of days just to get used to it. I was glad I wasn't going to be working with the animals.

We had had no training. We had to report to the depot next day. When we arrived we were given a tool kit, wrenches, spanners. I think first we were cleaning the machinery. We were shown the clutch and the brake on the tractor and off you went. We had to learn to put the blocks on if you were going on the road.

We worked from about eight till five but it depended on the time of year. We had Sunday and Saturday afternoon off. We all got on very well.

Soon after she arrived she went for a couple of weeks to Priddy with other girls to 'learn the insides and outsides of a tractor'.

From the depot at Temple Cloud she worked on farms all around Lansdown, Keynsham, Pensford, Stanton, Chew Magna and Nempnett Thrubwell:

Landgirl Violet Furmage, on a Fordson tractor c1943

The farms were mostly small. That was where the general agricultural workers went because the smaller farms didn't have the machinery. Sometimes I'd only go to a farm once.

We did ploughing, disc harrowing, rolling, turning the seed, mowing and thrashing (threshing). Thrashing was dusty work and towards the end the rats and mice would run out. The rick was surrounded by wire netting but the mice would get out. You were all right if you were wearing wellingtons; otherwise you were afraid of them going up your legs.

There wasn't always tractor work on and we would go hoeing. At haymaking and harvest we would work up until it was nearly dark. But we were paid overtime. It was hard work because I wasn't used to it but I stayed six and a half years.

Both women very clearly remember their uniform which was very different from anything they were used to, but they liked it and it was practical:

They used to supply us with some really good clothing. You had to send your measurements and the uniform all came by post. We were issued with two of everything and they seemed to last well but we could get more, as we needed them.

For work we wore all-in-one fawn overalls with bib and brace and in the warm weather creamy coloured short sleeved knitted shirts, like aertex shirts. In the winter we had green jumpers over that. We had brown overcoats like army coats but a bit shorter. But for walking out we had corduroy breeches and a very nice short coat in khaki, long woollen socks, a shirt and a tie, a green pullover and a hat. We had very good stout brown shoes, which you had to dubbin all the time to soften them up, and then your black lace up boots, and your wellingtons. I had never worn trousers before but when you are young you can more or less wear anything.

There used to be a song we sang:

> *'If you want to go to heaven when you die,*
> *Wear a green pullover and a tie,*
> *An old brown bonnet with WLA on it,*
> *If you want to go to heaven when you die'.*

Home Guard

Although there were representatives of every village in the valley fighting for their country by land, sea and air, the farming community and the miners in the local pits gave of their best on the home front. The Home Guard was an important organisation. Easy as it is to smile at what is often regarded as an amateurish 'Dad's Army', in rural areas they were not to be taken lightly. Many of them were young and fit farm workers or other men with vital everyday jobs. True in the early days they were untrained and ill equipped but they learned as they went. It was not a light matter to spend a night on guard duty when you had cows to milk morning and evening and be trained in manoeuvres and target practice on your day off! It should be remembered that if the worst had happened and a foreign army had occupied the country some members of the Home Guard would surely have formed the core of a resistance movement. Here is an account that underlines the dedication of these men:

During the day we were doing our normal job. It was only night-time and Sundays you turned soldier.

At first it was called Local Defence Volunteers, LDV.

It was based on Battalions and Companies and Platoons as the Army was and we had a Section here in Bishop Sutton but we were part of the Chew Magna Platoon. Second Somerset (Long Ashton) Home Guard Battalion. It was responsible for an area from the Bristol boundary to Priddy and from Felton to the A37.

Our Company Commander was a Major (Frederick) Terrell who lived at the top of Chew Magna. Captain Scott who lived in the Rookery, Chew Magna, was the Platoon Commander, and our Battalion Headquarters was Tyntesfield House at Wraxall. I started out as a dispatch rider when I was a Corporal and I used to go there and pick up instructions. Anyone who had a motor bike was a dispatch rider.

We trained in the British Legion Hall, the one behind the Red Lion, twice a week I think. That was training, arms drill. I started off with one stripe, Lance Corporal, Corporal, Sergeant and then Lieutenant. And I was then Weapons Training Officer for the Company. So I had to move around a bit then. I was quite busy. I had training at Taunton, at the Army Barracks. They used to get regular soldiers in, instructors, to instruct us who were going to be instructors. I think the Army regarded us as a bit of a nuisance. I don't think they thought all that much of us but I think probably the civilian population felt that we were doing a decent job though. We went on church parades with our rifles and stuff. I suppose it gave them a little bit of heart.

At first we would do three hours of a night twice a week and then later we would do all night duties, mostly on Knowle Hill Tump. We had an outpost there. We were mostly just watching and waiting 'cause at that time they were half expecting to be invaded anyway and we would have been the first people to have found out, I guess.

It was thought after Dunkirk in May 1940 that Hitler would invade the south coast and head directly north.

Good job he didn't. He would have walked over the British Isles in three weeks, I reckon. We had nothing. We started with pitchforks and anything you could get hold of, a good handle, a sledge hammer handle or something like that. Anything that you could protect yourself or hit someone with. And then also anybody who had a twelve bore or a gun of any description was allowed to carry it and carry ammunition as well. In fact we were supplied with a few cartridges. It wasn't very many but it was a bit. And then eventually of course we got proper rifles.

Chew Magna and Bishop Sutton Home Guard: (back row) Ryder, Bill Sage, ? , ? , Jim Harris, Clark, Osmond, Bert Bown , ? , Arthur Perry, Jeff Hasell, Tom Pearce, Bill Hasell, Roy Perry, ? , Bert ?, Trendall, Stephenson. (front row) Oliver Ware, ? , Jim Patch, Jack Marsh, George Perry.

But that was a good year before we got any.

You would probably do two nights of a week, all night. Soon as it was dark you had to be on duty at Knowle Hill Tump and then you would come off duty as soon as it was light. We had a Nissen hut at one time. I think it's still there, down over the Tump. I suppose there would be about twenty of us sleeping there when they were almost certain they were coming – after Dunkirk. They thought this was a good area where they could drop in with parachutes. You were allocated patrols and the rest were sleeping in the hut. Two on two off, or four off, all through the night from dark till daylight. It must have carried on for two or three years, I guess.

Then there were manoeuvres and shooting practice. We used to use Yoxter rifle range.

I nearly got killed once. We were doing grenade throwing. You were taught how to do it in a trench. Pull the pin out and you had a seven-second fuse or ten-second fuse on a live grenade. I think for practice you used a ten-second grenade. And we were down in the trenches somewhere up on Mendip, Gibbets Brow I think, and this chappy threw this grenade and hit the parapet and it came back in. Well of course he started scrambling out leaving me in there with this bomb with ten seconds to go. So I grabbed him by one leg and pulled him back and grabbed the bomb and threw it out at the same time. I could have been blown up then!

I think they probably disbanded the Home Guard as such fairly soon after the War but you could then go on reserve, which we did. I was on reserve for years and years. You didn't do training but your name was on a list and if they wanted you they would send for you.

Another volunteer simply couldn't wait to join the men:

I went into the Home Guard. I was in it but I wasn't seventeen, I think I was only sixteen or sum'it. And they said that I should be in the Cadets but I only had a few months to go and they said, 'Well, we won't say anything. Stay as you are'. I didn't want to go to the Cadets after being with the Home Guard, you know.

East Harptree had their own platoon, Litton had their platoon and Hinton Blewett had their platoon but we all three, we all came in together. West Harptree had Home Guard there but they came in with Compton Martin and Ubley, I believe.

We did shooting practice at Widcombe and we had a hen house. They lined it inside, closed the doors, and filled it with gas. We went in wearing the gas mask and the instructor put his finger underneath the mask so you could have a sniff, it wasn't very nice.

We used to do guard duty up at Nempnett. We had to walk up there naturally, and spend the night. We had a hut out there to watch for any paratroopers that were coming. We never had anything like that, thank goodness. But we were well prepared for them. We were quite well equipped towards the end with clothes and rifles. There was plenty of us in it. We all got on well together.

A former local policeman who was stationed near Taunton during the War has an amusing memory and we will end with his story. After all, that kind of experience and ingenuity could have come in useful!

They used to have Home Guard exercises where one battalion in a certain area would attack another. The South Gloucester force were to attack the Chew Valley Home Guard. So down at Taunton the police dreamed up an idea that they would send a Fifth Columnist into the area. 'What idiot can we send up there?'

'Oh, … he comes from Paulton area. He can talk the dialect up there.'

So they took me round to the barracks at Taunton and dressed me up into Home Guard uniform, they gave me a motor cycle but not before I had been drilled by the Chief Constable and his aides. They told me what I had to do. I had to go to my parent's home in Paulton. They told me I had to leave my parent's home on the motorcycle, come up over the Mendips and enter the West Harptree zone where the exercise was taking place. Now they said, 'You are attached to the Temple Cloud Home Guard, your Commanding Officer is Colonel Esherby and you have to take a message from the Colonel to the Chew Stoke Police Station'.

I was told who I was, what I was, that I was a Bricklayer and I worked for Johnny Knox in Bristol. Oh, they drilled me. They made sure I had it all done and dusted. What I was supposed to do was find the password for the evening.

So I came over the top of the Mendips and past the Blue Bowl, on the old road, and then you come to the Mill. Well I got as far as the Mill where there was several of the Home Guard there. So they said, 'Where are you going'?

I said, 'Oh, I've come from Temple Cloud Section, Colonel Esherby'.

'So what is the password?' this Home Guard asked me. I thought I was going to get dumped in the flipping mill.

'Oh, they never told me anything about a password. They just told me to take this here over to Chew Stoke Police Station.'

I can remember Wilf Simmonds of East Harptree, he was the Sergeant Major and he had a moustache out to here, saying to his Lieutenant, 'I don't like it, Sir. I don't like it, Sir'. And the Lieutenant saying to me, 'Now look here sonny, I'm going to ring up your Commanding Officer'.

So he did and came back and said, 'He doesn't know the password either!'

I said, 'Well, can I go on now'?

'No, I'll send you with an escort.'

I can always remember the bloke (the escort) *was always called Stumpy. He used to live at Chew Stoke. Stumpy, he wasn't as tall as the rifle. And he escorted me to Chew Stoke Police Station.*

When I got in there the Commander of the Police was there. I can remember the police officer at Chew Stoke was Johnson, he had a large moustache also, and I handed the message to him. He looked at it.

They questioned him. 'Well, I live at Paulton, Sir, but I'm attached to Temple Cloud. I've only just joined this Home Guard.'

'And what do you do?'

'Oh, I'm a bricklayer, Sir.'

'And who do you work for?'

'Johnny Knox in Bristol.'

'Oh, I know Johnny Knox. Oh, that's very good. Well done.'

And all the while this Johnson was there worrying his moustache and pondering over this message. Anyway he typed out a message and sent me off again with the message. And Stumpy was still outside with his rifle and at the pub at Chew Stoke he said, 'Are you coming in for a pint?'

'No, I'd better get on.'

Well we got up to where you go up to Breach Hill and there was a car there, two Special Constables and they stopped us. And I said, 'Do you know. I just joined the Home Guard at Temple Cloud and they sent me over here to Chew Stoke to deliver this here message. And there's a password. They never said nothing about this here password. I don't know anything about a ruddy password. What's all this password business?'

'Oh, you've got to have the password.'

I said, 'Well, I've to get back to Temple Cloud and I've got to go up over the Mendips and all the way round. But if I had the password I could go through the valley, the short cut'.

I said, 'I'll ruddy resign after this. I'm not going to have this nonsense. Can you tell me what the password is?'

Well they muttered between themselves. 'Shall we tell him?'

They told me.

I had then to go to Long Ashton Police Station and I can remember my Inspector from Taunton was there. He said, 'Do you know the password?'

'Yes, Sir.'

And I can remember the Inspector said, 'Put the bugger in the cells, put the bugger in the cells!' I did enjoy that but I wouldn't if I had been put in the cells!

Off duty

Social events formed a part in everyone's life when they were off duty. It was important for morale. The majority of the people involved were young after all.

During the War some of the halls were taken over. Bishop Sutton hall was taken over by Goldbergs the tailors. They were making uniforms there. We used to dance at the British Legion hall then. We used to ride our bicycles to it, blackout all around and lights all covered over. The local people used to fund raise for sending parcels to the soldiers they knew. And they used to have auctions. They had 'Salute the Soldier Week', I remember that one, and people used to give things and they sold them by auction. Mother bought a calf through that and we called it Soldier.

We used to have some very good concerts during the War because obviously people used to come out from Bristol. There used to be a couple, Mr and Mrs Kerr. They had a big garage in Clifton and they used to come out to sleep over-night to get away from the bombs and things and then go back during the day. They introduced a sort of concert party at the village hall and they were really quite good. It was mostly people from Bristol. And there was another concert party with a girl called Jean Hudson who was a marvellous tap-dancer and another one who was a tenor with a wonderful voice.

The effects of war

The two Great Wars of the 20th century were a major factor in the social changes that took place. The tight structures of the rural hierarchy began to crumble. Many of the farm families and workers were wrenched from their traditional homes and communities into a wider world that they often found challenging and exciting. In the long run this would have happened anyway. The drift from the land had begun a full century earlier but had now become a landslide. On the one hand new opportunities led to a more independent life style for most young people with better paid work away from home. At the same time they were often no longer needed on the farm. Shortage of labour during the wartime had combined with the drive for efficiency in food production to increase mechanisation. Without it small farms were uneconomic and they could not support a family. For many the world had changed forever.

It may seem strange to us nowadays that plans to flood the valley did not give rise to more organised protest, but at the end of the War people were accustomed to government direction and control. There was also the long established right of a landlord to end a tenancy at will. Faced by a compulsory purchase order in the case of their own farm, or a sale agreed by their landlord, they felt powerless and could only conform.

CHAPTER TWELVE

Building the Lake

Although construction of the reservoir did not begin until the 1950s, the need for additional water supplies, and the potential of the present site, had been recognised by BWW as far back as 1933-34, when Alexander Paterson was the chief engineer.

Plans and parliamentary approval

The first steps were: to construct a 'standing wave flume' gauge on the river near Chew Stoke; to set up rain gauges in the catchment area; and to analyse the water in the river. Trial borings were made at the narrow neck of the valley at Walley Court (the most suitable site for the dam) to assess the condition of the underlying ground.

When I was still at school we had five big Waterworks chappies come down from London and they stayed at Denny. They were planning how they had to measure the water.

I remember the rain gauges being erected and also men constructing what we called a weir – a sort of passage or concrete channel – to measure the flow through the river and that was monitored over many years. They built a little hut next to it and someone used to come down every day from the Waterworks.

The 'standing wave flume' gauge was also an attraction for the local children.

We went down there paddling and I had these new wellingtons on and I got in a hell of a mess. Tovey said, 'Let I have one of your wellingtons' and he went down to the river to get a wellington full of water to chuck over I and wash it off. He leaned down too far and dropped the wellington and down the river it went. I were in trouble then.

Other technical tasks carried out at this stage were those of preparing an outline design for the proposed reservoir and establishing a broad estimate of how much it would cost. The overall scheme included associated works, such as a pipeline to bring an additional water supply to the reservoir's pumping station from a source on the Winford Brook, but these are outside the scope of this book.

It was also necessary to establish who owned and occupied the buildings and the large amount of land that BWW considered it would need to acquire (by negotiation or compulsory purchase) for the reservoir itself and its immediate surroundings. Accordingly, a Bristol legal firm drew up a comprehensive schedule of information. This identified and described the use of each individual parcel of land – dwellings and farm buildings; whether fields were pasture, arable or orchard, and whether they included parts of rivers, streams, or ditches or were crossed by (public) footpaths, roadside verges, public roads and access roads to fields. The schedule shows who occupied and who owned each of these parcels at that time, and whether any others had financial interests. The latter were mainly the fishing rights covering almost all this stretch of the river, which were held by the Knowle Angling Association. The combination of this schedule with the accompanying large map of the area, that also identifies each parcel, provides a unique social record of this part of the valley in 1938.

In order to obtain the necessary Parliamentary approval for the scheme to build the reservoir, The Bristol Waterworks Company submitted a Bill to Parliament 'at the session of 2 and 3 George 6, 1938-9'. This is a lengthy document that includes the schedule of parcels and the associated maps. The essence of the scheme, as contained in Clause 9. (1) (a), was to make and maintain in the rural district of Clutton:

A Reservoir (to be called The Chew Stoke Reservoir*) in the parishes of Chew Stoke, Chew Magna, Compton Martin, West Harptree, East Harptree and Hinton Blewett or some of them to be formed by means of an embankment across the River Chew commencing in the parish of Chew Stoke in the enclosure numbered 262 and terminating in the parish of Chew Magna in the enclosure numbered 931 on the Ordnance Map Second Edition 1902 Somerset Sheet XII. 14...

*(It was not until a competition was held by BWW in 1954 that the reservoir acquired its present name of Chew Valley Lake.)

River Chew sluice gates 1946/47

The Bill was passed and became an Act of Parliament in 1939. The way was now clear to proceed. However, WW2 and the more urgent priorities of the post-war years meant that the scheme had to be put on hold.

Getting the go-ahead

Water consumption continued to increase and, in 1947, BWW was given permission to construct a temporary intake and pumping station near the proposed site of the dam at Chew Stoke. This supply was connected into the 'Line of Works' aqueduct built in 1846 to carry the water to the treatment works at Barrow.

The reservoir scheme was eventually sanctioned in 1949, following a government survey of water in the Mendip area. The survey recommended that the scope of the scheme should be increased so that the reservoir could also supply the additional needs of some smaller water undertakings. The building of the treatment works at Stowey was a significant addition to the scheme to meet these extra obligations.

Obtaining the sanction for the scheme was the trigger for the more detailed design and tendering processes, leading to the appointment of contractors for the construction of the reservoir and the various associated works, such as roads and houses. The negotiations for acquiring the land and property needed were also started. These are discussed later on under a separate heading.

The contract to construct the reservoir was awarded in 1950 to A E Farr & Co. ('Farrs'); a family firm originally founded in Hereford but based at Westbury in Wiltshire by the 1950s. The firm had been carrying out civil engineering contracts in Bristol from soon after WW2, clearing up the legacy of the war years and contributing to the rebuilding of Bristol. Their work included the demolition of public shelters for Bristol Corporation in 1946, and roads and sewers and other infrastructure for the housing estates at Henbury and Hartcliffe.

Building the reservoir

Work started in November 1950 with building a road to the site of the dam – including widening the first part of Walley Lane. The objective was to complete the reservoir by 1955. It was also hoped to start extracting some water for use by 1953, once the reservoir had started to fill sufficiently. Construction of the dam was clearly critical to achieve this.

Apart from works associated with the main dam, the other main civil engineering works were concerned with providing new roads and subsidiary embankments to carry these. The lanes crossing the lake area were stopped up. The present road across the dam and round the north-east side of the lake was built to connect Chew Stoke and Chew Magna (via Denny Lane) with the lanes to Bishop Sutton. A temporary road diversion was needed for a couple of years until the road over the dam was ready.

Parts of the road from Chew Stoke to West Harptree were below the top water level of the lake (the 185 ft contour line) and so the section of the road between Stoke Villice and the turning to Nempnett and Ubley was realigned further to the west.

The engineer who designed the new Chew Stoke to West Harptree road section was a keen motorcyclist. He designed the camber on the bends so that on a motorcycle you could take the bends at high speed and accelerate into the straight.

The embankment at Herons Green, which carries the new road, was needed to protect the large area of low-lying land to the west from being flooded. The streams and ditches carrying water into the Chew at that point were intercepted higher up the slope by catchwaters (ditches and aqueducts) that discharge their water into the reservoir above high water level.

For similar reasons, the section of the West Harptree to Bishop Sutton road at Herriotts Bridge, where the Chew enters the reservoir, needed to be realigned and raised on an embankment. This straight section replaced a bend in the road where it crossed the original Herriotts Bridge, which is remembered as a hazard to unwary motorists.

Within the enormous area of the reservoir itself, the sad but necessary tasks of demolishing buildings, and clearing trees and hedges had to be carried out. It was noted how the clearance changed the microclimate and made the valley windswept and significantly colder. Stratford Mill was dismantled and re-erected at the Blaise Castle Museum. Materials from some properties were reused and timber from the larger trees went to the sawmill – the cedars from Denny 'Hills' Farm being used for the first Woodford Lodge. The archaeologists worked against time and the rising water, to investigate and interpret the Roman and earlier sites uncovered by the construction machines. Clutton District Council built houses at Chew Stoke for some of those who had lost their homes, and BWW built five houses at points round the reservoir for their employees who would look after it. Last of all, trees were planted and the surroundings of the reservoir landscaped and fenced to lay the foundations of what can be seen today.

The maximum number of people employed on the construction was said to be around 300. As well as local people, others were brought by bus from Bristol and Bath. Working hours were officially 8 am to 5 pm with overtime up to 6 pm, if needed – although the buses to Bath and Bristol left at 5 pm. Payment was weekly and the notice period was two hours.

Cedars of Lebanon Denny 'Hills' Farm 1952/3

Farrs were advertising but I was going to Priddy Fair and I met Frank Morgan (General Foreman with Farrs) and I said, 'What about a job? Start today'. And he said, 'No. We never start in the middle of the week but come Monday morning I'll see you then'.

Although he said that he wanted work as a driver, he was initially put to work on digging the trench for the foundations of the dam, which had previously been stabilised by injecting concrete into the cracks in the bedrock. The concrete filled trench is located deep down below the pavement beside the road over the dam.

Well I went in there. They couldn't get men to go down in that trench. One time they give them all a rise but we didn't get a rise so old Stan Chidzey from Sutton, he said, 'Right, let they go down for a week and we'll come up on the sunshine'. And he went up and saw the head bloke and he said, 'No, they won't go down in there'. Stan said, 'Well, we want more money.' So we had more money than the men on the top.

I was in the trench for twelve month digging. They weren't never allowed to blow it because you'd make some cracks, wouldn't you. A year before, they bored holes and injected concrete in to fill any little cracks. When we were in they trenches you did see it, the seams were filled up with concrete. Then afterwards they did put this trench right the way through. We went down about 30 or 40 feet. Up the top end, towards Chew Stoke, that was the hardest stone. That was just like drilling and we had to take that out with jack hammers or down with pack (pick) and shovel. There were little cranes with Lister engines on they, and they drop a bucket down in and they take the spoil out.

We worked in water. The stream was still going through but they put the stream up a lot higher so that they could get through this trench. What they done were put some big irons in along where the water was going through. We did go in at seven o'clock in the morning and get wet through 'cause the water would be dripping.

One night they had a hell of a flood and that stream busted through and that stream went back on its same track. It took wheelbarrows, everything with it.

Of course they had pumps going day and night down in the trench. The night shift had to keep that trench dry all the time or else it would be flooded next morning. They had big diesel pumps for there. Well of course, a pump will push the water miles but he won't pull it so you had to have the pump and smoke down in that trench with 'ee.

If the pumps had to be attended to at night, the men had to climb down the timber bracing in the trench. This and several other potentially dangerous situations were recalled:

Construction work at Chew Valley Lake 1951

They never had no ladders, down there. They put the diesel ready for night time to fill it up and you had to get up and down there at night. A lot were half afraid to go down 'cause there weren't no lights much. No Health and Safety in those days. No compensation if you got hit. That was it.

Me and Stan Chidzey went on some of the holes to be like a foundation on the Chew Stoke side with a small trench. Then when the bucket with the dirt were going up you had to get back in and under because in case that ruddy rope broke you'd have had it.

Not many was injured. There was no first aid on the spot at all. There was one I took to hospital, he'd cut his hand when they were mixing the cement. There was nobody there to do it. They come down and asked me to take him to hospital because I had a car.

Down there by the pump house one day Farrs had to go down and dig a trench. Well this chap didn't realise electric wires were up over. Of course he swung the ruddy bucket round and all caught on the wires. All went flash, the ground were on fire. He were ruddy lucky he weren't electrocuted.

I tipped two dumper trucks over at different times. I tipped the dumper over up on the top with a load of concrete. The ground was uneven where these big tractors go through. And I tipped one over coming back from Stratford Mill. He hit the bank and went over and old Darby come out and said, 'I thought I seen your mess along the road'. Darby was a boss with Farrs but he didn't stay very long. He was a bit of a bloke; he had a spy glass and from that top office he could look all round to see everybody.

No special protective clothing was provided – many wore the army battle dress that could be bought then – 'You got given your wellingtons and all the tools was there'.

Farrs and BWW both had their site offices where the pair of Water Works houses above the pumping station are now. That was also where concrete was made in big mixers and then transported to the trench.

They had a track (railway line) *which did go right down through with the cement in buckets. A crane had to pick those buckets and lower it down into the trench. Loads and loads of proper cut timber ran through the trench with very strong sheets of metal shuttering top to bottom on the sides holding the sides from coming in. When we did concrete we did pull that out only a little way and keep on coming up.*

On top of the concrete, the core of the dam was made of puddled clay, nearly all of which was taken from near Stratford Mill. The clay was mixed with sand in a twin-shafted pug-mill near the site offices, where the concrete blocks to face the dam were also made.

We did bring the clay back and tip it up. There be three of us hauling it and that had to go up an elevator, through the machine. It would come out in a long line but a bloke with a spade would be there cutting it as it came out in blocks. Then into a Fergie trailer and that had to be took down to where they were putting the clay. The blocks had to be placed clean in a layer in the trench; there would be two or three blokes throwing it and then they had to make heel marks all over that in proper lines. That was where all the work came in. We didn't call it puddling.

The banks had to be made up in thin layers and they had to go over it rolling it with holes in the soil and then they did water it. There was a tanker there. Every load had to be rolled properly 'cause the Waterworks people would be there watching. Out where the teashop is now, that's where they got all the dirt from for the embankment. I know one or two people who did drive the 'happy wagons' – the caterpillar tractor (the D.8 tractors pulling trailers of red marl for the bank fill). *When they did go on to that bank they could tip either side. They had a lever in there to pull as they drove along. In the summer time when they did stir up the dust, you could see the dust for miles. And you would come home covered red.*

The concrete blocks to line the embankment were made up at the site from moulds and they had to be let down with a crane.

Frank Morgan he was a good general foreman, he were everywhere but he were fair. One day I was coming back through fields with some clay and he jumped on the side, but they (the workmen) couldn't see, and they started throwing clay at one another – well you got like a hundred men like! He was clever and he went down and said, 'Come on chaps, we busy today', (the sun was shining). And they cussed 'e and that. And Frank said, 'Never mind, I can't sack them today but I got 'em marked for when we get wet weather.' They were straight up the bloody road! (Laid off when the weather was bad.)

There were some good carpenters and other craftsmen working on the reservoir but others tried it on. At Herriotts Bridge, for example:

All those stones put in there was numbered. They were brought there perfect; each stone had to be put in perfect and you had to go over there and find what number they want. That were a proper stone mason from Chew Magna, I just did the fetching and carrying.

Well of course in them days you didn't have to have no papers (qualifications). *...they think, 'I could earn more money', stay away for a week or two and come back as a carpenter with a hammer. They were ruddy hopeless. Morgan did say, 'I seen your faces before'.*

I was there when they were doing the clearing. Minto (later Ubley sawmills) *had most of the trees. Walt Goldstone was down there with a little Fergie cleaning up the hedges and they were burned. They had to cut all the hedges off not to have too much dirt and burn all the brash. You could drive straight across with the dumpers and the tractors from Herons Green to Hollowbrook. You could drive anywhere.*

Afterwards when all the men was finished I laid all the ground down for them, all round the sides, every bit, with a pair of discs and a little Fergie. I done all the fields down towards the lake and then a lot up towards Breach Hill because it was all where they'd been working. I did all the verges. I just disc harrowed it and two others did put the seed in. I did work me own hours at the end because the disc harrow was there and Garrett and Frank Morgan didn't take no notice. I used to whip back to Ubley, milk two cows and go back at night.

Ray Walker did do all the banks. He could make the banks level with a crane. His father and his other brother laid all the sides of the banks going over from Chew Stoke this way to Harptree and Bishop Sutton with turf. The turf was cut from down on the lake from different fields.

Some petty theft as well as more serious pilfering of materials took place, particularly lead which was expensive and in short supply at the time.

Every night, wherever we were working, he did go home with a shovel or a pack (pick) on the bike. We did say, 'Are you taking it home'. And he'd say, 'No, not for nobody to pinch it'. When he died he had a ruddy shed of they packs and shovels and the handles had all rotted over the years.

And then there were the houses they pulled down and an awful lot of lead used to go off the roof. We're not mentioning any names! Of course the Waterworks were blaming our men like for pinching the lead. Old Frank Morgan said, 'Where do you reckon that lead's going?' I said, 'Well, see the lorry what coming in and out here two or three times a day. Pull 'ee up and stop. Don't blame our folks'. Well I think they did give him a warning. And of course one of them what did work for him did live at Regil and he fell off his motorbike one night and there was lead all over the road.

Working on the construction of the reservoir had its advantages.

I was only getting £6 a week when I was on the farm. When I finished up driving for them I was getting about £16 a week. I didn't like it at first – not for a long time – but when you go and take your money you think, 'This is better than on the farm'. And oh, cor we had a lot of fun. A lot did moan but they did seem to stay there.

Some people worked in the site office.

He was my boss, Mr Garrett. I worked for him for three years. It didn't bother me being the only girl in there. Of course it was very convenient to just walk up the road. – no travelling. The only thing I didn't like was having to work on Saturday morning from 9.30 to 12.30. I used to think that was a waste because you could have had a whole day to yourself, not go in for three hours.

I was happy working there. I had my own office. I remember sometimes Mr Garrett would be dictating a letter to me and someone would burst into the office – something would have happened down on the site. He would just have to drop everything and run out and I wouldn't see him perhaps until the next morning.

They were supposed to have very good wages in those days. I used to help put the wage packets up and the labourers they earned three times as much as the office workers. The best (paid) of the office workers were the clerks and they were getting £8 and the labourers were getting up to £20. That were a lot of money in those days.

I didn't come into contact with any of the labourers at all. I never left the office. Only on one occasion Mr Garrett wanted to take me down to the site. There was 200 men working down there. I felt really embarrassed. I didn't really want to go but he insisted. Down in that trench, it was mud everywhere. They had the stream ducted over them and the water was falling over them. They were always working in water.

Property acquisition and dispossession

Once the go-ahead had been given, BWW representatives and Mr Barwick, Clerk to Clutton Rural District Council, met the farmers concerned in October 1949, at the temporary pumping station at Chew Stoke, and explained the plans for land acquisition (by compulsory purchase) and for the construction of the reservoir. By this time, BWW had already purchased some of the properties – for example, Chestnut Farm in 1940 and Yewtree Farm in 1948. The next generations of these families occupied them as BWW tenants.

Compared with the types of protests that might be expected nowadays over a project requiring such a large amount of land, there appears to have been relatively little active protest, either at an official or popular level. Certainly there is little evidence of this from parish council minutes. Someone who was not directly involved suggested one possible reason:

I think they just took it for granted. I can never remember hearing of any protests whatsoever. Today they would all be up in arms. Quite a few of the farming families were put in other farms and because of that it was fairly peaceful. Houses were built in Bushythorn Road, Chew Stoke and many people were rehoused there.

There had been an attempt to oppose the original BWW Bill, however:

My Grandfather led a deputation of farmers, who owned land that was to be requisitioned, to Parliament to lobby all the MPs, because it was to be done under an Act of Parliament... but of course he lost in the end.

The younger generation may have had a different view to their parents.

We were always under the impression that they were going to make the lake and then the War came. I grew up knowing my home was going, we didn't think about it as kids.

The veteran local journalist Eldred Walker – whose family had occupied Whitehall Farm for a period during the 19th and early 20th centuries – campaigned against the scale of acquisition and demolition.

I remember Eldred Walker, a very outspoken journalist, and I can always remember him standing up at the meeting and having a real go... He said, 'I believe that Bristol Waterworks have taken this opportunity to purchase land cheaply around the area which they do not need. And I am going to take this further.'

Whatever the rights and wrongs of this assertion, no doubt views and technology had also changed in the twelve years since the plans had been drawn up in 1938. For whatever reason, the end result was that several properties originally identified for acquisition were left standing and are still occupied.

Spring Farm at Sutton Wick was a most interesting historical building that stood well away from the water. Those that knew it could not understand why it had to be demolished, and the general feeling was that, in the present day, it would probably have been saved.

Compensation was paid to the owners based on the value of a farm according to the practices of the time.

> *Those farmers were only paid the value of the land and nothing else, whereas now you would get consequential loss, loss of income, loss of profits and all sorts of things. Back then you were just paid so much an acre – house thrown in – and off you go.*

Many farmers were tenants rather than owners and their compensation was based on two years' rent. As rents were generally low, so was the compensation.

Having to leave one's home under those circumstances was difficult and emotional. Some farmers were able to buy farms or obtain tenancies, in the area or further afield (one going as far as New Zealand). Others were not so fortunate. Several families moved into the recently built council houses at Chew Stoke.

There were compensations, however, as one girl who moved with her family to Chew Stoke remembered:

> *I can't recall a particular time when I knew we had to move. I think it drifted*

Demolition of Woodford House 1951/52

up on me. I should have remembered it with great sadness but I think I remember it with excitement – electricity, my own bedroom, things to do of an evening, youth clubs. I joined the youth club straight away. I joined the bell ringing. I joined the dancing club. I was out every night but there was always homework. I moved from there with excitement and I didn't look back. But the flipping cats went back so we had to keep going back.

The archaeologists were perhaps the last temporary inhabitants, camping out in the last buildings to be demolished and using a boat to reach the sites still workable on the higher ground. Appendix B gives details of the more permanent owners and occupiers.

As the people left and the water rose, the wildlife was already starting to arrive.

Lots of coots were breeding there, hundreds and hundreds. The only rare one that came was a Marsh Harrier.

Some of the men digging the trench was waiting for a duck to get too near... it was a dinner! And Dick Brew used to have duck shoots when the lake were being filled.

The inauguration

The inauguration of the Chew Valley Lake on 17 April 1956 by Queen Elizabeth II was a great occasion locally and many people remember the event – almost all the school children were taken there. The Farr Family Chronicle also recorded that this was 'the outstanding event of 1956 in the context of our business'.

I took a load of East Harptree kids to the opening. I think the whole school went.

The Queen! I was there, I had just come back from Germany. I can remember sitting on the bank and the car came along, and she was only about from here to there. I had a really good view. Everybody was there.

We were invited. I had a bluey, not actually navy, suit with spots on and navy hat. We had food in a marquee.

My three children were all home with chicken pox. Rather than mix with the crowd by the dam we went to the two places where the royal car had to slow right down. We went to the hump-backed bridge by the fire station in Chew Magna and by the sharp bend at Hayes Pond Corner, on the A368 by Sutton Court, so we could have a good view of the Queen and Prince Philip. At the latter site Prince Philip pointed out our two Labrador dogs to the Queen.

Many of the people involved with the construction of the reservoir were presented to the Queen and there were displays to watch. The inauguration site

Inauguration of Chew Valley Lake 17 April 1956. Sir Foster Robinson Chairman of Bristol Waterworks Co. presenting W Cox to HRH Queen Elizabeth II, W G Monk, J Collins, F Flower, F C Morgan, W Warren, C Trendall, and M Weeks were also presented.

near the dam was of course decorated with flowers to look its best. People particularly remember the primroses on the bank. They had been specially dug up and transplanted from the banks and lanes round Bishop Sutton, and were returned to where they had come from shortly following the Queen's departure!

The reservoir was not completely full until 25 February 1958, even though the works had been officially commissioned on 23 December 1954 and the pumping station at Chew Stoke was fully operational by January 1955. The aim of abstracting some water for use in 1953 had certainly been achieved by September 1954 when abstraction was halted for a few months to enable installations to be fitted to the main valve shaft and the tunnel through the dam.

By the time the inauguration ceremony was held, the lake was already becoming established and starting to enter its new role as a place for recreation as well as a source of water.

Postscript

Leaving the farms and cottages that were lost to the lake caused varying degrees of sadness to all those who had spent most of their lives in the valley. The young had grown up with the knowledge that at some point it would all come to an end and not only they but all the community would move on.

The tenants of some small farms and cottages of course looked forward to the modern and convenient homes provided by the local council. Others, who perhaps were in a better financial position, succeeded in gaining the tenancy of another farm a little further afield or were able to invest in a place of their own. Much depended on having marketable skills and qualities. In some cases, the lake itself gave employment. Nevertheless some people were almost heartbroken and expressed a sense of grief and loss of the life they had to give up.

In many ways the new reservoir only served as a catalyst in this area to highlight and bring into focus changes that were occurring countrywide. Divisions of labour between parents and children, males and females, which had been part of a traditional way of life, were no longer acceptable. The survival of small family businesses may have depended on them but times were different at the end of WW2. The small valley farms and way of life would have changed regardless of the flooding of the valley; it only hastened the inevitable.

Not every aspect of change is however, negative. Young people in the area had far brighter prospects in some ways than previously. It is surely a significant point that at this time the educational centre of the whole valley became the newly built Chew Valley School. The new school opened in 1958 as a secondary modern so that, in the beginning, children were still being selected for places at grammar schools in neighbouring towns. But the school was fortunate to have a dedicated and forward thinking leadership and the support of practically the whole community. So much so that just over a decade later the school achieved 'comprehensive' status thus providing post eleven education for all valley children. At first it was to be named Chew Magna School, until it was pointed out that most of the site was in the parish of Chew Stoke. Then it was agreed that, as with the new lake, it should be given a name that reflected the whole of the catchment area.

Children of secondary age came to it from all the villages around and it not only raised academic expectations but it also became the focus of their social interaction. They came from a range of backgrounds but they had at that time one thing in common, an understanding of rural traditions and the values of their community. New friendships were formed across the valley by youngsters who shared a variety of common interests. These ranged from sport to social activity. As personal transport became easier they were often free to visit each other's homes in their leisure hours. There were frequent party invitations from their early teenage years. In this way the younger generation widened their circle of friends and became attached to a wider community and many of them still are.

From the beginning, BWW had intended to develop the lake as an important and prestigious fishery and preparations had been in hand, well in advance. The grounds were being landscaped, shelter belts planted and reed beds were growing around the shallow fringes. Using Blagdon as a base, trout were bred to stock it and attempts were made to clear the waters that flowed into the reservoir of coarse fish. Landing stages and fishing boats were introduced and the first fishing lodge was built in the Woodford area where licenses and tackle were to be sold. The lake opened for fishing in 1957 and quickly became immensely popular with local fishermen as well as attracting anglers from all over the world.

At this stage nature herself took a hand and wildlife colonised the new wetlands. There was an influx of wild geese and various breeds of duck. Other waterfowl soon recognised a new resource. Migrating birds discovered a welcome stopping place and took full advantage of it. Rarities began to crop up from time to time, bringing eager birdwatchers in their wake! There were waders, and a variety of hawks, and the reed beds were home to coots and moorhens. Less often seen than heard, a number of warblers were there too for the waters were enriched by the insect life and decaying vegetation that was drowned by the rising waters. Swarms of midges and other flies hatched on spring and summer days. These were an unexpected nuisance to local people as is evident from items in the newspapers at the time. Various ingenious means were attempted to reduce the problem but the trout also fed on them and quickly grew to a great size. Bird hides were provided and ringing stations. Sir Peter Scott came from Slimbridge and worked with local naturalists, and even some local children were encouraged by him to take an interest. Already the lake was bringing great joy to hundreds of people. A television recording first shown in 1971, 'Man Made for Nature', exists as a record of these early days.

Other groups also identified the value of the new lake for recreational purposes. From the earliest days of its creation there had been repeated requests from the local dinghy sailors such as Pegasus the Uphill based club (British

Aeroplane Company works club but also open to non employees) to allow sailing on this new inland water. For some while it was felt that sailing, with fishing and wildlife interests on the same stretch of water, would be incompatible. Finally however, with the encouragement of Denis Howell, the first Minister of Sport, a compromise was reached. Chew Valley Lake Sailing Club was formed to sail in fishing's closed season and was established on its plateau on the west side of the lake, just to the north of Woodford Lodge. Sailing started in December 1967 with a membership of 130. At first the club was housed in a wooden hut but after two or three years the season was extended, though the summer sailing area was restricted. A new clubhouse was built, more slipways added and a membership of four hundred allowed.

Local schools used it on one day a week and there was an RYA training programme. A class and handicap racing programme was established and the club hosted regular Open and Championship meetings as well as the Schools County Regatta and even to many non-sailors the sight of a race in progress is an added pleasure. However, it did admittedly take some years before understanding and tolerance was fully established between sailors and fishermen.

In 1972, the first picnic and car park areas were constructed to accommodate the general public. The ground on the eastern end of the dam was landscaped and first a visitors centre, toilet block and a snack bar were built. Later when this proved so popular a very pleasant café was built. In addition an area further to the south, was developed, complete with nature trails. The whole of this side of the lake is a most enjoyable viewing area, as are the lay-bys at Herriotts Bridge and Herons Green. Finally, at Woodford Lodge a restaurant has been added completing the amenities and accessibility to the lake scene.

The Chew Valley has seen many changes in its long history of human settlement. These last fifty years since the creation of the lake are but a brief period in its evolution. Whatever the arguments against the flooding of a pretty and productive valley it cannot be denied that man with nature has produced a beautiful and priceless asset.

APPENDIX A

Ownership of Whitehall Farm in the 18th Century

In 1788 Mr Bentham of Lincolns Inn in London was asked to give his legal opinion on the title to the Symes estate in Chew Stoke and to advise a potential purchaser on the parties that would need to be involved in its conveyance. The abstracts of the documents he was given relate to what was to become Whitehall Farm and cover the period from the beginning of the 18th century. Quite apart from the complexities of 18th century property law that they presumably present, they tell us who owned and/or occupied the property, who provided money on mortgage, and who acted as agents or executors holding property on trust or had other interests.

The property in Chew Stoke that was the subject of these transactions did vary over the years – for example, in 1771 there was a newly erected dwelling house and the acreage was slightly reduced. For most of the time, however, it was described as a tenement or stall house and about 31 acres of land – in three closes called Valley Meads, two closes called Cow Leazows, three closes called the Upper Ridings and Ox Leazow and two closes called Redfields. This land was bounded to the west by the lands of Richard Leversedge and to the east by the lands of Thomas Bilbie and Henry Fisher. It had been part of the demesne (that is directly farmed rather than tenanted) of Walley Court in the manor of Chew Stoke.

In 1700 William Webb a yeoman of Chew Stoke took out a 99 year lease on the property, which he left to his daughter Mary in his will on condition she settled some of his debts. Accordingly, in 1714, after his death, it was arranged that William Webb of Breach Hill (probably Mary's brother) should hold the lease in trust for Mary and her intended husband, Richard Heale, a 'victualer' of Chew Stoke, and pay off the debts.

In September 1718, Richard Heale, now described as a yeoman, also bought the manorial rights to the same property in Chew Stoke for the remainder of a 1000 year term, which the late Gabriel Odingsells, lord of the manor, had sold with other manorial rights in 1705. The purchase price of £120 was actually paid by Joseph Lane a yeoman of Chew Stoke, who thereby held a mortgage on the property from Richard Heale.

The heirs of Gabriel Odingsells were his son Gabriel and daughter Mary, married to Samuel Morley. They were similarly faced with settling their father's outstanding debts out of their inheritance. Possibly because they lived in London, or because a certain Peter Davis of Wells now held the remainder of the '1000 year term' to the manorial rights, they commissioned two citizens of Wells to arrange the sale of sufficient assets to clear the debts – including the sale to Richard Heale. These were Dr Claver Morris and Richard Comes. Dr Morris was the well-known diarist who is buried in Wells Cathedral and Mr Comes appears several times in his diary in connection with official business – perhaps he was a lawyer.

Richard (now described as a butcher) and Mary Heale held and occupied the property for another ten years – re-mortgaging it twice along the way, first to Samuel Paine of Bristol and then to Mary Norcot a widow of Winford.

In September 1728, they sold it for £460 to John Lukins of Chew Stoke. John Lukins also bought with a mortgage, this time from John Goodhind the Elder of Whitchurch. The reason for the sale may well have been that Richard and Mary Heale did not have any children. William Webb also included in the same sale the remainder of the 99 year lease that he was holding in trust for them – on condition that £100 of the £460 should be paid over to Robert Ricketts of Stowey and John Hasell of Stanton Drew to the particular use of Mary.

John Lukins and his wife Judith occupied the property for 25 years until, in 1753, they settled it on their daughter Mary and her husband to be, John Plaister of Wrington. It appears that the Plaisters probably did not occupy the property as only one year later, in 1754, John Plaister sold it for £525 to his tenant James Dando, a baker of Chew Stoke, under a mortgage held by Thomas Abraham of Compton Martin. The property was remortgaged in 1766 to William Cox a yeoman of Pagans Hill in Chew Stoke.

In October 1769, James Dando (now described as a yeoman) 'in consideration of the natural love and affection which he had towards his daughter Mary Symes wife of Samuel Symes' (a victualler of Bristol) releases 'a dwelling house, garden, orchard, barn, stable etc, and two pieces of arable land' to Benjamin Roynon, a shoemaker of Chew Stoke, and Thomas Stokes of Bristol, in trust for the use of Samuel and Mary.

Some legal agreements over the next couple of years appear to refer to property transactions and mortgages that are not solely concerned with the 31 acres previously involved, and introduce as other parties Alexander Adams of Houndstreet, Marksbury, William Bush of High Littleton and George James of Chew Magna.

By October 1771, however, we are back on familiar ground, with Samuel and Mary Symes taking out a mortgage of £500 with Tobias Peters a yeoman of Chew Stoke 'for all that newly erected dwelling house with the stall house adjoining and 23 acres of land'. This comprises the 31 acres less the closes called Redfields.

This mortgage was outstanding when Tobias Peters died before September 1778. He left instructions to his two executors to let it run, with the interest payable to his wife until her death or remarriage, and then to call the mortgage in for repayment for the benefit of his daughter. Nine years later, in 1787, it was still outstanding when William Wallis, the last survivor of the two executors, died. He was survived by his wife and by his son, who was under age. This was the situation as it stood when the request for the legal opinion was made.

APPENDIX B

Who Lived Where

Property	1901 Census (At house on census day)	BWW 1938 Schedule Occupier (Other Owner)	Last Permanent Occupier	Additional Comments
Walley Court	Thomas & Caroline Stowell, sons John, Edward, William & James, and a married daughter Elizabeth Chancellor	Edmund Keel & Frederick Keel (Somerset County Council)	Keel families	Edmund's family moved to Winscombe, Frederick's moved to Chew Stoke.
Woodford House. There was also a cottage in the grounds.	1. Plant? & Lidia Atkinson, sons Robert & Joseph daughter Florence. Elizabeth Feltham a housemaid. 2. Benjamin & Bridget Atkinson, son Ronald, daughters Lizzie, Edith & Gertrude. Phoebe Maisey a mother's help.	Louis Conway.	Mr & Mrs Conway (Norman Wilson lived in the cottage from 1948.)	The Atkinsons all came from the North of England. Only Elizabeth Feltham was born locally.
Whitehall Farm	Victoria Walker and her son Eldred. Emily Pale a domestic companion.	Walter Read.	Read family	Walter & Lilian Read retired to Breach Hill. Nelson & Dinah Read moved to Shoreditch Farm, Chew Stoke

Denny Farm	William & Octavia Hasell, daughters Hannah, Mary & Alice, sons John, William & Wilfred. Florence Maggs a domestic servant and Jane Vowles a nurse.	William Hasell.	Hasell family	The Hasells moved to Woodbarn Farm, Denny Lane
Cottage between Denny & Denny House Farms	John & Emily Durbin, daughters Bessie & Lilian, sons Henry & Frank.	A ruin by 1938		
Denny House Farm	George & Mary Mapstone, son George, George Mapstone a relation. Alice Sawell? a domestic servant, John Chapman farm worker.	Edmund Mapstone.	Mapstone family	The Mapstones moved to Dorset.
Denny House Farm Cottage	James & Jessie Clark, daughter Mabel and son Francis.	Richard Williams (Edmund Mapstone)	Williams family	The Williams moved to Chew Stoke
Denny 'Hills' Farm	Edward & Sarah Bryant and son Arthur.	Ralph Hill (Arthur Penny & Denis Harward).	Hill family	Bowyers had the farm before the Hills. Both families moved to Mendip.
Chew Park Farm	James & Kate Baber and visitor Lily Popham.	Reginald Lyons (Francis Weetman).	Stokes family	Reginald Lyons moved to Lower Gurney Farm
Chew Park House	John & Emma King and daughter Sarah.	Frederick Ashford.	Mrs Ashford	Mrs Ashford went to her son at Yeovil
Spring Farm	Edward & Anne Baber, daughters Maude & Hilda, sister in law Eliza King.	William Hasell (Katharine Hunt).	Hasell family	See Denny Farm
Mead Farm, Chew Park Lane	Thomas & Jane Bendall, sons George, Arthur & Wilfred, daughters Ethel, Elsie, Dora & Gertrude.	Jane Bendall (Mary Phelps).	Mellish family	
Cottage 1, next to Mead farm	Robert Barrett, his mother Ann, sister Hannah and brothers Stephen & William.	Solomon Mail.	?	
Cottage 2, next to cottage 1	John & Sarah Wright.	Minnie Vowles (Archibald Webb & Percival Webb).	?	
Herons Green Farm	Henry & Priscilla Maggs, son Sidney and daughter Lily.	Lily Holbrook (nee Maggs) (Jerrard Hunt).	Mrs Holbrook and the Patches (her children by her first husband)	Patch family took over Moat Farm as tenants of BWW

Herriott's Mill House	George & Ellen Baker, and sons John, George, Rees & Clifford.	Ivan Gay (Duchy of Cornwall). Mill disused.		Ivan Gay lived at Lower Gurney Farm.
Stratford Mill & House	Arthur Hassell, his brothers Maurice & Percival, and sisters Florence, Edith, Eva & Vivian. Frederick Cole a corn miller.	Arthur Wilson & Alfred Gay (Duchy of Cornwall)	Wilson family	The Hassells ran the mill from 1861 until 1930. The Wilsons moved to Ubley Hill House
Stratford Lane cottage	William & Emma Randall and son Gilbert	John Loveridge.	Loveridge family	In c1928 Ben Chapman lived here.

Hamlet of Moreton

Moreton Farm	Emily Cole (widow of Edward Cole) and sons Edward, Walter, Arthur & Henry	George Curry from c1920. (Ashton Hunt).	Curry family	Ted & his parents went to New Zealand, then Herons Green Farm. John farmed locally, then near Wells.
Laurel/Cross Farm	William & Dora King, son Edgar. Laura Pitman a domestic servant and Albert Fry a farm labourer	Edgar Sims, from 1929.	Mr & Mrs Sims. Sold to BWW in 1951.	In c1920 Arthur & Ernest King, then c1926-28 Mr & Mrs West farmed here.
Chestnut Farm	William & Charlotte Keel, their son Walter Keel, nephews Elsworth Roynon & Clifford Keel, nieces Amy Stowell, Elizabeth King & Annie Keel, and cousin Emily Heal.	James Stowell owner from 1920. Sold to BWW in 1940.	Reginald & Amy Marshall (*nee* Stowell) and family	The Marshalls moved to Breach Hill, Chew Stoke
Yewtree Farm	George & Eliza King, their niece Gertrude and George Pulham a farm labourer	Clara Maggs. Leonard & Clara Maggs from 1923. Sold to BWW in 1948.	Brian & Vera Maggs	George Pulham was at Moreton Farm in 1891. The Maggs moved to Chew Stoke in 1952.
Grove Farm	George and Emma Cole, sons George, Joseph & Lewis, and daughter Mary	Lewis Cole (Sarah Keel). Also here c1920.	Whitfield family (Mrs Whitfield was daughter of Lewis Cole)	The Whitfields moved to Chew Stoke.
Moreton House, on lane from main road	Unoccupied property in 1901 census(?Note 3)	Arthur Derrick (Arthur Penny & Dennis Harward). Here from c1923.	Derrick family (temporarily Tibbs family from Stoke Villice)	Also known in 1950s as Tibbs Cottage.
Next cottage on lane from main road	Leonard & Clara Maggs (? Note 3)	Mary Marshall (Sarah Keel)	Chubb family	In c1928 Lionel Small and family lived here. He worked at Chew Park Farm.

Moreton Farm cottage 1	George & Jane White, their sons Theodore & Herbert (?Note 3)	William Powell (Ashton Hunt)	Jack Tucker and family	In c1926-28 Harry Fry and family lived here. He worked at Moreton Farm. The Tuckers moved to Chew Stoke.
Moreton Farm cottage 2	Unoccupied(?Note 3)	Unoccupied(?) George Curry (Ashton Hunt)	George & Mrs Tucker (parents of Jack Tucker)	In c1928 this was let to the Compton family.
Moreton Mill House, cottage 1	Emily Head, son Charles, daughters Edith & Beatrice (? Note 3)	James Vowles	Unoccupied?	In c1920-34 the Goldstone family lived here.
Moreton Mill House, cottage 2	Only one of two cottages mentioned in 1901	Unoccupied	Unoccupied?	

Stoke Villice from Chew Stoke to lane to Herons Green. Property descriptions are as BWW 1938 schedule

Cottage on left	George & Emma Holland, and son Frank(?Note 3)	William Stockwell	William Stockwell?	
Cottage on left behind previous one	Brothers Henry and Frank Edgell (?Note 3)	Herbert Chapman (William Stockwell)	Tibbs family?	
Cottage on left	William & Sarah Smart, daughters Jane & Edith, and son Frank.	Sarah Smart	Stevens family?	
House on right	Not yet built.	Herbert Voke (Albert Voke)	Herbert Voke?	Mr Voke was a builder & built this house
Bungalow on right	Not yet built.	Frederick Cole (Walter Cole)	Ray Cole?	
Bungalow on right	Not yet built.	Lister Irvine	? See note 2.	This was a wooden bungalow on stilts.
House on right	Not yet built.	Herbert Redwood		

Note 1. *Several other properties were included in the BWW 1938 schedule for compulsory purchase but were not demolished when the reservoir came to be built. In some cases the whole of a farm property was originally going to be purchased as it would no longer be viable once the majority of its land had been taken. However, where the farmhouse itself was away from the lake, the house was retained. In other cases the passage of time led to second thoughts. The properties concerned, with their occupiers in 1938, are (going clockwise round the lake): Knowle Hill Farm (Richard King); Twycross (Herbert Chapman); Rockleaze (Henry Dagger) and four dwellings nearby in the lane to Bishop Sutton (William Vowles, Edward Williams, William Withey and Thomas Webb); cottages at Stitchings Shord Farm (George Cole and Ephraim Veale); Wick Farm (George Panes); Manor Farm (Clement Gay); Lower Gurney Farm (Ivan Gay); house on Chew Stoke to West Harptree road south of Moreton junction (George Marsh); farm at Herons Green, now called 'Herons Green Farm' (Ernest Hobbs) two dwellings at Stoke Villice west of Chew Stoke to West Harptree road, now called 'Lake Side' and 'Lake View' (Frank Martin and Ernest White).*

Note 2. *Opposite this bungalow was a building that was first a milk depot and then a fertiliser factory, which included an asbestos bungalow that was lived in by the Wilson family in 1934/35. The factory was derelict by 1938.*

Note 3. *It is not possible to be absolutely certain who in 1901 lived in which one of these dwellings at Moreton or Stoke Villice that are marked '(?)' because the number of inhabited dwellings in 1901 differ slightly from those recorded in 1938.*

Where the Artefacts Went

The BWW Newsletters of the 1950s refer to artefacts and features of demolished buildings that were to be given for safekeeping to museums and other organisations.

Those items that have been traced during the research for this book are listed here.

Chew Stoke Parish Church

The remaining parts of Moreton Cross have been re-erected in the churchyard.

The statue of the lady with an anchor from above the door at Walley Court, and the stone spy hole or ventilation shaft from the cellar there, are both in the porch.

Bristol City Museum

All the Prehistoric, Roman and Medieval pottery and other objects found during the archaeological dig are held here.

The large beam over the inglenook at Mead Farm was also said to have gone here but has not yet been traced.

Blaise Castle Museum

Stratford Mill has been re-erected in the grounds. Three apple tree trunks from Yewtree Farm were used to repair the mill machinery.

Apparently, it had been the intention at one time to construct a farm and a tithe barn at the Blaise Castle Museum using artefacts and features from various buildings, but this did not happen. Those items at Blaise from the list below marked (*) are currently held in store and are not on display. The other items listed appear on the museum central register but had not yet been traced by the museum staff.

The oak dresser from Walley Court.

From Denny House Farm, an iron lock (*), two beams from the barn roof, six harness racks, two sections of cow stalls, the iron latch from the cowshed door and the front door (*). The fanlight from this door is apparently in store at the Industrial Museum.

The roasting jack from Denny 'Hills' Farm (*).

From Chew Park Farm, an old internal door, a stone finial, two beams from the old kitchen and one beam from the sitting room.

From Yewtree Farm, the front door (*), a gun rack and twelve oak beams (possibly for reuse elsewhere).

Other Locations

Keys from several of the demolished buildings are displayed in the Bristol Water Museum at Blagdon Pumping Station.

Some items that would otherwise have been lost are in private hands.

APPENDIX D

Abbreviations Used, Bibliography and References

Abbreviations used

BRO – Bristol Record Office
BWW – Bristol Waterworks Company Limited
OS – Ordnance Survey
SA&NHS – Proceedings of the Somerset Archaeological and Natural History Society
SRO – Somerset Record Office
SRS – Somerset Record Society
WRO – Wiltshire Record Office
WW2 – World War 2, 1939-45

Bibliography and Main Sources Consulted
(not referenced again in individual chapters)

'Excavations at Chew Valley Lake, Somerset' by P A Rahtz and E Greenfield, Department of the Environment (1997) for all information on pre-Roman, Roman and medieval sites and discoveries. Also references to some original documents. (Chapters 2, 3 and 4)

BWW Newsletters, mainly 1949-56, are the main sources for the construction of the reservoir, descriptions of buildings demolished, artefacts found, and related stories.

'The Bristol Waterworks Company 1846-1946', by Frederick C Jones (reprint 1993), 'The Story of the Bristol Waterworks Company 1939-1941', by A Hodgson (1991) and a typewritten document by W J Williams of BWW were also consulted for those chapters about water supply and the reservoir construction (Chapters 4 and 12).

The BWW Bill submitted to Parliament 1938-9 (SRO Q/RUP/684) is the source of information about owners and occupiers of buildings and land expected to be compulsorily purchased for the reservoir construction in 1938.

Census returns for the parishes of Chew Magna (Bishop Sutton), Chew Stoke, Compton Martin (Moreton) and West Harptree for 1901 and some earlier dates, local directories, and electoral rolls are the official sources for who lived where and when.

Chapter 3 Anglo-Saxons and Middle Ages to 19th Century

'*Some Domesday Manors*' by S C Morland in SA&NHS Vol. 99 (1954); and '*Victoria County History of Somerset*', for information on Domesday Book.

'*Burci, Falaise and Martin*' by Sir Henry Maxwell Lyte in SA&NHS Vol. 65 (1919) for information on these families.

'*The Moreton Effigy*', a paper by the Compton Martin Parochial Church Council, for information on Thomas de Moreton.

'*Exchequer Lay Subsidies for 1 Edward III, 1327*', in SRS Vol. 3 (1889), for the tax levied on John de Moreton and on Petrus de Santa Cruce.

'*Descent of the Gournays of Somersetshire*' by Daniel Gurney (c1841), for documents witnessed by the de Moretons. Also for information about the Gournays.

'*Register of Bishop Ralph de Salopia*', SRS Vol. 9, for licence of the chapel of St James' at Moreton.

BWW photograph album for window of ecclesiastical building found at Grove Farm.

'*History of Somerset*' by J Collinson (1791), for the holding of Moreton Manor by Sir Matthew Gournay and his wife Alice.

'*Somerset Enrolled Deeds*', SRS Vol. 51 (1936) & '*Sales of Wards 1603-1641*', SRS Vol. 67 (1965), for documents concerning Jane Still.

'*The Story of Compton Martin*', compiled by Marion Wareing (c1954) for some information on Moreton Farm.

The extract from Joseph Leach's c1850 visit to Moreton Farm was found in a newspaper cutting of probably 1950s in a private scrapbook.

Map of Eleven Miles Round Bristol by B Donn (1769) for references to occupiers of Walley Court, Woodford Farm (House) and Chew Park (Farm).

Transcript of letter from Philip Rahtz (c1951) in SRO Ref. DD/X/MAY 19, for description of Walley Court.

'*Sir Walter Raleigh*' by Raleigh Trevelyan (2002) for information on John Gilbert.

'*Calendar of Some Medieval Manuscripts in the Custody of Bridgewater Corporation*', SRS Vol. 57 (1942) for the Gilberts and the Le Waleys.

'*Somerset Medieval Wills (1383-1500)*' edited by Reverend F W Weaver, SRS Vol. 16 (1910) and '*Somerset Wills from Exeter*', SRS Vol. 62 (1952) for references to Veales and Fishers of Denny.

'*The Diary of a West Country Physician, A.D. 1684-1726*', edited by Edmund Hobhouse, (1934-5) for Dr Claver Morris and Mr Comes (e.g. 24 June 1720).

Privately held documents for ownership of Whitehall Farm in the 18th century.

Blinman papers in BRO, for conveyance, Robert Blinman Dowling to John King, 1845.

Western Daily Press, 24 December 1955, for story about Edward Baber.

Lease dated 1714 at Heron's Green (Herring's Green) is in SRO ref. DD\BR\wh/4.

'*Old Mendip*' by Robin Athill (1964) for information on turnpike roads.

Chapter 4 Mills and Early Water Extraction

Martin Bodman kindly allowed us to make use of material that he had accumulated about mills on the Chew. We also consulted his article 'Mills of the Upper Chew' published in the Journal of the Bristol Industrial Archaeology Society, for information on the mills from Chewton Mendip to Shrowle. In this article he references an unpublished paper 'Watermills of the Chew Valley' by A J Spence as the source of some information.

'*Warp and Weft*', by Kenneth A Rogers, for information on the cloth industry.

'*Paper mills in Mendip/North Somerset*' in Somerset and Dorset Notes and Queries Vol. XXV, 1947-48, for paper mill at Herriotts Mill in 1816.

'*A Brief Glimpse Into the History of Bishop Sutton and Stowey*' compiled by Jill Tovey, for the information about George Arter and the mill at Stowey Bottom.

'*The African Trade and the Bristol Gunpowder Industry*', by Brenda J Buchanan, in Transactions of the Bristol and Gloucestershire Archaeological Society, Vol. 118, 2000, for information on resiting the gunpowder industry, including to Moreton Mill.

Compton Martin parish records for information about the accidental deaths of Thomas Urch and Joseph Gaskell at Moreton.

Will of Sarah Dowling of Stratford Mill, 28 November 1789, in SRO ref. DD/SASS/C/82/9.

Will of John Collins (of Stratford Mill), 7 November 1822, in BRO ref. 39203

Somerset Box 1 location 2EE58.

Extract from a letter received from Rev. G Shipman-Fox of West Harptree Vicarage about John Collins and 19th century owners of Stratford Mill (Yeovil Public Library and Museum, 14 October 1949).

'*Grandfather Hassell's Mill*' by Mary Noble in *The Listener* 13 May 1954 and '*Celebrating Grandfather*' by Mary Noble in *The Lady* 7 September 1961 for information about the Hassell family of Stratford Mill.

'*Notes from Interview with Thomas Broad, Miller at Stratford Mill 1942-46*' by D J Everleigh (1 June 1988), for information about Vowls & Handcock Ltd.

Chapter 5 A Walk Round Moreton in 1938

'*The Story of Compton Martin*', compiled by Marion Wareing (c1954) for an additional eyewitness description of Moreton in 1953.

Chapter 10 Social Life and Entertainment

'*Sales of Wards 1603 – 1641*', SRS Vol. 68, 1965 for information on fishing rights on the Chew held by the lord of the manor of East Harptree, Sir Theodore Newton.

Chapter 12 Building the Lake

Farr family papers in WRO (ref. 2233/220/1) for information on A E Farr & Co.